DATE DUE

My Own River Kwai

PIERRE BOULLE

My Own
River Kwai

Translated from the French by
Xan Fielding

NEW YORK

THE VANGUARD PRESS, INC.

My Own River Kwai

CONTENTS

FOREWORD

I have tried in these pages to recall as faithfully as possible some personal adventures in the Far East through which I had the good fortune to live in the course of the last World War: a past which is already distant in Europe, a prehistoric era for the South-East Asia in which these events are located. But there have always been devotees of prehistory.

These memoirs start at the declaration of war, when I was working as a rubber planter in British Malaya (the peninsula of Singapore or Malacca, for the benefit of those who, like myself, have neglected the study of geography). The first part covers a period of 'normal' mobilisation in Indo-China, whither I had been summoned like many other Frenchmen. It is pretty monotonous. I have cut out a fair amount of tedious episodes and have retained only what is necessary to ensure the continuity of the narrative.

It was only after July, 1941, when I returned to Singapore and joined Free France, that events took a more exciting turn for me: for me and a few others, mostly planters, a small group of Frenchmen exiled at the other end of the earth and kept in a permanent state of restlessness by the equatorial sun, the upheavals in Europe which we followed feverishly every evening on the wireless and also, it must be admitted, a natural tendency to impetuosity and ebullience, the very tendency perhaps that had drawn us to Malaya in the first place. We were romantics.

We were romantics! The course of the war, the series of disasters that had overwhelmed our country, assumed in our eyes an element of wonder that was even more fabulous and

7

tragic for anyone listening to the news in a plantation tucked away in the middle of the jungle, and cruelly conscious of his isolation and helplessness. It is therefore not surprising that when the war spread to South-East Asia our first reaction was a feeling of hope: at least we were not to be eternally excluded from the epic. Nor should it be held against us that our ambitions were exaggerated and that the schemes we contemplated hardly tallied with our capacities. We were romantics: amiable, touching, bumptious and probably incurable romantics.

This narrative, as I said, bears upon 'personal' adventures, and perhaps I should apologise for this. Many other people in those disturbed days experienced stranger adventures, adventures that were more dashing, more glorious, and above all more useful and more closely connected with the historical march of events which these memoirs do no more than touch upon as occasion offers. (I am thinking in this context of the brilliant part played by Francois de Langlade throughout this period, a part to which I have only briefly alluded; likewise of the clandestine activity undertaken in Cochin-China by Bocquet and one or two others, an activity which manifested itself in the destruction of an impressive tonnage of Japanese shipping.) But in describing these I should have been carried away and I don't feel I am qualified to write an historical work.

Apart from the question of egoism, which prompts any individual to take a close interest in what has happened to him in particular, I have a special reason for unearthing these memoirs, written shortly after the end of the war, and for giving them a title which alludes to one of my novels. Indefatigable snoopers keep asking me where I drew the inspiration for this book, *The Bridge over the River Kwai*. For a long time I vainly tried to elucidate this mystery, which was as irritating for myself as for them. If the source of the *details* is obvious, where on earth could I have found the general idea, the *background*, which to me is essential?

Well, I believe I have solved the problem. The background is likewise contained in this series of adventures. It is there implicitly; it is not perceptible at first sight. I did not know this myself and became aware of it only after several years of anguished introspection.

It would be tedious to go into the mechanics of the transposition. In these pages I merely give the *narrative* after the *novel*, while stating that the one contains in a diffuse state all the material, all the spiritual substance of the other. This, more than any real explanation, will perhaps shed some light on my intuitive conception of the art of fiction.

P.B.

Indo-China
1940–1941

I

MALAYA

For us planters in Malaya, the declaration of war was preceded by a period of intense over-excitement due to the expectation of serious events and an over-indulgence in whisky. The Tamil coolies, the Chinese houseboys, the Malay drivers who occasionally endured the backlash of this nervous tension (we were high-handed overlords, frightful colonialists, perhaps) followed its progress with ever-increasing apprehension and every evening discussed its latest tiresome developments.

Our irritability was aggravated by exile and the inability to participate at once in the drama which we knew was unfolding and which, under the equatorial sun, assumed even more extravagant proportions than it really had. We would brood every night on the latest news bulletins. When war broke out we felt almost relieved. We fondly thought we would be recalled to France in the very near future.

September, 1939

I was then on the Sungei Tinggi plantation, some fifty miles from Kuala Lumpur, the rubber capital. Like everyone else, I prepared for a departure which we all considered imminent. Mobilisation of the French was undertaken through the good offices of our consul in Singapore. He had written telling us to be ready to move off at short notice.

I had two large cases built by a Chinese carpenter, into which I packed the crockery, books and knicknacks that encumbered my bungalow. I had the sensation of making a

13

clean sweep of the past. I saw myself already far, far away from the plantation.

October, 1939

The consul's summons failed to arrive. We began to feel irritable again. I found myself spending a major part of the day and night listening to the wireless, together with the director of the plantation. False rumour succeeded false rumour. San Francisco announced that the Siegfried line had been pierced and the French armies were breaking through into Germany. The report was denied the following day.

November, 1939

The consul in Singapore at last decided to attend to us. Barbier and I, two of the youngest, were called up and posted to Indo-China, the assembly point for all the French residing in this vast sector which included Malaya, the Philippines, Indonesia, China and even Australia. Others were to join us later.

There was a big farewell party at the local club-house in a palm-tree plantation. We were treated like heroes. The drink flowed; French and English sang in our honour *For He's a Jolly Good Fellow*. The Malay drivers listened outside, squatting on their haunches.

The next day I had my packing cases nailed down and left them in a warehouse on the plantation before setting off with Barbier for Kuala Lumpur. We said good-bye to de Langlade, the director of the company, who watched us leave with a touch of nostalgic envy. His duties kept him back for the moment, which was not much fun for him in the present atmosphere.

At Singapore the consul received us with a monocle screwed into his eye. He noted with a sigh that times were hard and his funds limited, that he couldn't refund us our travelling expenses from Kuala Lumpur to Singapore—not that we had even asked him to!—but that he nevertheless considered it his duty to stand us first-class tickets from Singapore to Saigon.

This question of funds seemed to be his main concern at the
moment. He stressed the point again and apologised for having to make us travel on a small cargo boat, the *Maurice
Long*, on which the fares were less expensive than on the big
liners. We took leave of him, without pointing out that in the
Maurice Long, which was assigned particularly for the transport
of pigs and dried fish, there was neither first nor second class.

After an uneventful three-day voyage we reached Indo-
China and steamed up the Saigon River between dreary
marshy banks, with egrets flying overhead, which reminded me
of certain corners of the Camargue.

2

COCHIN-CHINA

On arrival at Saigon our luggage was examined by a Customs official from Martinique, which went against the grain. (We were frightful colonialists.)

The consul having omitted to tell us to whom to report, we went along to Army Headquarters, where a tubby little staff captain looked at us in bewilderment.

'You've come from Malaya? ... Kuala Lumpur? ... What the devil are you doing here? Weren't you all right where you were? ... Well, we'll see what we can do for you. Meanwhile you may as well look in on the Gendarmerie.'

The Gendarmerie sergeant had never found himself in such an embarrassing situation.

'Kuala Lumpur, you say? ... Malaya ... Malaya? But what the devil are you doing here? I've no instructions at all ... You'd better go along to the Garrison Orderly Room.'

At the Garrison Orderly Room we found another tubby little captain. This one openly commiserated with us.

'Just between ourselves, now'—he gave a wink—'what are you up to here? A funny idea to send for you all the way from Malaya. You'd better report to the Transit Camp. I'll ask Hanoi for orders.'

This went on for two weeks, during which we exhausted the pleasures of the Cochin-Chinese capital. We were not the only ones. Saigon was overflowing with reserve lieutenants like ourselves, newly mobilised, who spent their time in the cafés in the Rue Catinat or the night-clubs of Cholon waiting for the authorities to give them a posting. This was the fourth month of mobilisation.

One morning, at last, we had a call from Headquarters. We were being dealt with. Barbier was sent off to an Annamite light infantry regiment stationed at Thu-Dau-Mot, which he was to leave a little later on being transferred to the Air Force. I was posted to Saigon itself: 2nd Colonial Infantry Regiment, 3rd Company, Captain D.

Captain D. was a good-natured man. He gave me the picture straight away.

'I'm not hard to please, you know . . . Turn up in the morning. Try to be on time for parade. After that, if you have anything to do in town . . . well . . .'

At five o'clock next morning I was nevertheless on parade. There were three men in the ranks and a sergeant, who solemnly presented them to me as 'the company'. There were a few more, he informed me, but they had been detailed for fatigues; he didn't know exactly where they were. Next day things began to look up: there were seven men on parade. But subsequently there was no one left but the sergeant, and he too finally disappeared. There was nothing left for me to do but saunter down to the Rue Catinat for breakfast or else while away the time in Captain D.'s office by giving him a detailed account of life on a British plantation, for which he was infinitely grateful since he was bored to tears.

After a week of this programme I received notice to transfer. Someone at Headquarters having observed that I was a former motorised cavalryman, I was posted to the Saigon Armoured Cars Detachment. I reported to yet another captain. This one looked extremely annoyed.

'Are you really so keen on joining the Armoured Cars? Pity. I know another subaltern who would suit me down to the ground. If you wouldn't mind . . .'

He was like a horse dealer trying to strike a bargain. I lost my temper. I told him I didn't give a damn for his armoured cars and had only come here because I'd been told to. He wasn't at all angry. On the contrary, he looked relieved.

'In that case everything will be all right. I'll see to it straight away. You'd better go back and wait for further orders.'

That very afternoon I was again transferred and posted to an Annamite light infantryman regiment. Here the men did come on parade. Rather too many of them. There were not enough quarters for them all. They were kept busy all day building bamboo huts. I felt as though I were back on the plantation supervising the work of the coolies.

This lasted no more than four days, however, for I was once again transferred and posted to the Military Training Centre at Mytho, a small Cochin-Chinese town surrounded by paddy fields and situated on the banks of the Mekong some fifty miles south of Saigon.

January, 1940

This time it looked more like business. I remained a whole month at Mytho.

The Training Centre consisted of about a thousand natives recruited from all over the provinces through the good offices of the Cochin-Chinese officials; they were labelled 'volunteers'. In point of fact each province had had to produce a quota laid down by higher authority and it was pretty certain that some pressure had been exercised by the *tri-phus,* or native headmen. A few of these volunteers deserted on the very evening of their arrival.

They were quartered somehow or other in the schools and religious institutions which were scattered all over Mytho. I was put in command of St Joseph's School, a benefice of the Annamite Fathers, into which over two hundred men had been crammed. The school was divided into two halves, one for the riflemen, the other for the children. In the evening the Fathers would come and catechise the soldiers.

I was mainly engaged on teaching them how to march in

step and shoulder a piece of bamboo in lieu of a rifle. I sadly reflected that my friends in Malaya had celebrated my departure for the wars and were picturing me at this moment en route for the Maginot Line.

Since marching instruction still left me ample leisure, I had a little canoe built by a Chinese carpenter. In the evening I would go for long trips down the Mekong (which at Mytho was as wide as an arm of the sea), to the great concern of the garrison commander, a nice fellow who never ventured to administer the mildest rebuke but in whose eyes I discerned unvoiced reproach. What a terrifying number of nice fellows one encountered among the officers of the Colonial Army who were unwilling to cause the slightest offense to their fellow-men!

Time passed slowly, occupied by training, trips on the Mekong, games of bridge in the club with the doctor, the justice of the peace and the director of the Public Works department. It was the dull little life one might lead in any French provincial town in peacetime. I was not sorry to hear that I was to be transferred once again and sent up north to Annam: to Hué, to be precise.

3

ANNAM

It was twenty-four hours by rail from Saigon to Hué, but the discovery of the Annam coast alleviated the length of the journey. Nhatrang, Cape Varella and the Bay of Tourane had an almost Mediterranean aspect.

After the usual orders and counter-orders, the military authorities sent me to Phu-Bai Camp, some ten miles from Hué, on the Mandarin Road. In the bamboo barrack rooms of Phu-Bai Camp there were five thousand Annamite riflemen, in theory all volunteers like those at Mytho, but in actual fact conscripted through the *tri-phus* from among the poorest of the peasants. I was amused to hear how the camp came to be created, according to a Commie-minded colleague who told me the story on the evening of my arrival.

For a long time the military authorities had been looking for a convenient spot in which to quarter these thousands of riflemen enthusiastically recruited throughout Indo-China since the declaration of war. One day a staff officer walking in the country came upon a huge sandy space without a single tree, blade of grass or drop of water. Without a moment's hesitation he decided this was the ideal site. In this way, apparently, was Phu-Bai Camp created.

There were twenty or so officers here, almost all of them draftees and including a lot of 'foreigners', as Headquarters called us Frenchmen residing in Malaya, Indonesia, Shanghai or Australia, and summoned like myself to Indo-China. The most recent arrival was Louyot, another planter from Malaya, who gave me the latest news from there.

20

The training programme was the same as at Mytho. I was beginning to get fed up with this and could no longer muster the enthusiasm I had felt at the start. It was obvious these worthy peasants would never make soldiers. Was it really worth expending so much energy on teaching them how to handle a rifle?* In any case, a rifle was as much of a rarity here as at Mytho, for the time being at least, and marching in step still constituted the basic training: arduous training for these poor fellows who had manifestly never worn shoes. The few Annamite corporals who were here had a rather original method of instructing the recruits. They would make them stamp hard with the left foot. Apparently this was the only way of achieving a semblance of unity.

It yielded curious results. At dawn every morning, by which time the temperature at Phu-Bai was already almost unbearable, these children of the Annam paddy fields could be seen marching up and down the roads and tracks in columns of threes, their apprehensive faces almost hidden under outsize helmets, their skinny bodies clad in uniforms intended for Senegalese riflemen, raising the left foot and bringing it down in a cloud of dust as if their very lives depended on it.

March,1940

Time passed slowly. A small group of officers, to which I belonged, had asked to be sent to France as soon as possible, but there was little chance of our request being granted. We felt as though we had been sentenced for life to marching instruction. This was reflected in our keenness in our work. We slackened off, took rooms in the big Hotel M. at Hué and deserted the straw huts of Phu-Bai as frequently as possible to spend the night in town. Hué had a special, unforgettable charm, with its broad avenues flanked by flamboyants, its

---

* On re-reading these notes, it looks as though I was much mistaken on this point (as on many others). They have learned how to fight since those days—against us. Or maybe they weren't the same men?

native city where the loveliest girls in Indo-China seemed to congregate—girls with long hair flowing down to their shoulders, tall and slender compared to the plump little Cochin-Chinese—its rolling countryside covered in pinewoods, its hills sheltering the tombs of the emperors of Annam, its river, the famous River of Scents, dividing the Annamite town from the European quarter and seething at nightime with converted sampans on which were available all the traditional pleasures of pre-war colonial life. As for the scents, one had to travel upstream well away from the town before one could get a whiff of them.

The imperial palace overlooked the river. Occasionally, in the park, one could see the huge elephants which the present emperor kept like religious relics. His Imperial Majesty himself never moved except in his big sports Delahaye or personal plane.

I noticed incidentally that there seemed to be two emperors at Hué: the monarch of Annam and Monsieur M., who owned more or less all the hotels and cinemas in the region and controlled most of the local commerce. I always felt the latter exercised far more real power than the former.

April, 1940

A hot wind sometimes blew through Phu-Bai Camp. It was the famous Laos wind, which dried up one's throat and raised clouds of choking white dust that seeped into all the hutments. The water problem became really serious. Drinking water was delivered from Hué in barrels and we had to travel several miles for a bath.

At last we were issued rifles: one to every three riflemen in the more favoured units. They were Russian weapons, stamped with the hammer and sickle, and said to have been confiscated in France from Spanish Republicans crossing the frontier.

The rifle range was anything but a health resort. Whenever

a round failed to detonate (which happened fairly often)* our worthy riflemen would look heart-broken and try to clear themselves of responsibility. Their immediate reaction was to brandish the barrel of the loaded weapon in the face of the corporal or sergeant, just to show them there was something wrong and that it wasn't their fault.

May, 1940

As an interlude, I was sent to Northern Annam to take a census of all the horses up there in the event of a possible requisition. (I never managed to find out if the plan was to eat them or send them to the front in France.) It was my qualifications as a former cavalryman which earned me this honour. That I was merely a motorised cavalryman and knew nothing about horses didn't matter. I was careful not to raise any objection.

I drove around in official transport for a fortnight or so in the company of a veterinary officer who, thank heaven, had been attached to me. We went right up into the mountains and visited a number of isolated villages in the provinces of Vinh, Than Hoa and Ha-Tinh. The natives would bring their horses along to some pre-arranged assembly point. Some of them apparently travelled nearly a hundred miles to answer this appeal. I thus made my first acquaintance with the mountain races of Indo-China, who bore no resemblance to the lowland Annamites. These were Muongs and I took to them straight away. My only criticism of them was the horrid brew, sucked up from a jar through a long bamboo, which they felt obliged to invite us to share and which was the filthiest poison I had ever tasted, even after sampling various examples of Chinese rotgut.

The horses they produced were scarcely larger than goats. Even without the vet's advice I would have pronounced them unfit for military service. I always suspected the Muongs

* This remark is not intended as a denigration of Russian weapons. The round would fail to detonate because we had been issued ammunition of a different calibre.

of having made a careful selection before bringing these animals along. They knew I wouldn't travel a hundred miles on foot in the mountains to make sure there were no others.

I got back to Phu-Bai just in time to witness an official ceremony: the departure for France of a contingent of our riflemen. They had been issued brand-new uniforms and even scarlet belts twelve inches wide. Drawn up in columns in front of the train which was to take them to the embarkation port, they waited in the blazing sun to be inspected by a general and by the Emperor, who had been invited for the occasion.

I looked at their faces, almost hidden under helmets which were new but as usual too big. Their morale didn't seem very high. Some of them looked resentful, others tearful. Clearly, the 'volunteers' were wondering what was happening to them and felt far from reassured. Some of their families were there as well, milling round the train. The expression in the women's eyes was frankly hostile.

The Emperor eventually turned up, together with the general. He was dressed in a yellow robe in which he was clearly ill at ease. He carried out a rapid inspection; then the riflemen were bundled into the train as quickly as possible so as to cut short an unpleasant scene. For by now the volunteers were blubbering like babies. The women jabbered at us; what they said was incomprehensible but certainly not complimentary.

At last they were off. All told, it hadn't been too bad. In some camps, apparently, entire families had lain down on the rails in front of the engine. The vague unrest I had felt soon disappeared. We headed for the mess, where a little reception had been organised for the Emperor, who seemed relieved the official ceremony was over. The general made a speech, addressing him as 'Sire', and thanked him for allowing his subjects to contribute to the defense of our country.

This contingent of riflemen never got to France. A few days after their departure, the Germans invaded Belgium and Holland. The depressing atmosphere of the Phu-Bai desert, the enervating one of Hué, were suddenly charged with electricity. Feverishly we resumed our sessions round the wireless.

June, 1940

France had collapsed—a tragedy which none of us expected, except for a few pessimists who were told to shut up. Waiting for the news became more and more agonising. With difficulty I deciphered an announcement, relayed from London, by a general named de Gaulle.

The mess-room, after a period of gloomy despair, now resounded with heated arguments. There were some who talked of leaving Indo-China secretly by way of Burma and making for British territory, but nothing came of this. I personally couldn't make up my mind. Happy are those who are always able to make up their minds. I have known four such people in my life, maybe five. I admire and envy them.

July-August, 1940

Our uncertainty was aggravated by the attitude of Japan, who now redoubled her threats and provocations on the wireless, and by the mystery which still hovered over the intentions of the civil and military authorities in Indo-China.

Japan began by requesting us to close down the Yunnan Railway, one of the two supply routes into China (the other was the Burma Road, which was now beginning to be widely discussed and had always fired my imagination). Japan was also said to be making more substantial demands.

As for our authorities, for a time it looked as though they were going to put up a show of resistance. The first Japanese demand had been met, but there was a rumour that General Catroux, the Governor General, was negotiating an agreement with the British for the defense of Indo-China. A colonel had assembled all the officers at Hué and informed them of the High Command's decision not to recognise the armistice. We received orders to pick out the best units at Phu-Bai and organise them into commandos. A new wave of enthusiasm swept the camp. For several days we devoted ourselves to route marches in the mountains, maneuvers in the jungle and the lagoon.

This didn't last long. General Catroux left Indo-China and was replaced by Admiral Decoux. There was a noticeable change in the tone of the press. People began to come out in their true colours—not for the best from my point of view. At Phu-Bai some officers saw fit to remove the Union Jacks decorating the mess. There were some hard words exchanged, and even blows. The atmosphere became unbreathable. Phu-Bai Camp was finally wound up.

September, 1940

The Lang-son incident: a Japanese army marched up to the Tonkin frontier and demanded admittance into Indo-China. Negotiations, orders, counter-orders. In the end the French Government yielded. Meanwhile—and apparently as a result of some misunderstanding, for the agreement had already been signed—there was a bit of a scuffle at Lang-son, which ended for us in complete defeat.

By now it was more or less obvious that Indo-China favoured the Vichy Government. I was beginning to think more and more of Malaya and to work out more or less hare-brained schemes to get back there, when the Siam incident occurred.

4

LAOS

October, 1940

The incident started only a few days after Lang-son. For us it manifested itself first of all in vague rumours about the threatening attitude of the Siamese on the borders of Laos and Cambodia. They were apparently demanding a rectification of the frontiers.

Since the winding-up of the camp I had been transferred to Hué, to the A.M.D. or Annam Motorised Detachment, a somewhat grandiose term to designate two motorcyclist squads and four rather ancient armoured cars (the same vehicles which had been used for the famous Citroen Expedition of 1931 but fitted with light armour-plating). I had been put in charge of these.

The A.M.D. was the first detachment to move to Laos in order to oppose the Siamese demands. I received orders to lead the way with my armoured cars and (a bit of luck) a small civilian sports car. The prospect of this trip made me shelve my harebrained schemes. Maybe it was not very glorious, but there it was: the thought of discovering a new country called Laos outweighed my feverish concerns of a patriotic nature and my lengthy meditations on the subject of duty. My first reaction, when I learned of the decision to move, was to buy a shotgun and a supply of cartridges, since Laos was said to be good game country. There it was and I couldn't help myself.

My main anxiety now was whether my ancient motorised

vehicles would stand up to a two-hundred-mile journey. They acquitted themselves quite well, however, apart from losing an occasional rubber tread from their tracks. The men of the A.M.D., handy men by nature, always managed to make some improvised repair in spite of having no spare parts. At the end of the trip the tracks looked rather like shoes that had been resoled, but they still worked.

As for me, I drove those two hundred miles in the sports car some distance ahead of the column, admiring the picturesque mountain road (linking Dong-Ha to Savannakhet) which plunged into wilder and wilder country. Maybe it was not a very orthodox formation for a vanguard, but I thus escaped the monstrous cloud of dust raised by my caravan. From time to time I would let a driver take a turn at the wheel, so as to be ready to shoot down any game that appeared on the way, in the absence of a German, Japanese or Siamese. But it was still too early in the season; the wild fowl had not yet emerged from the forest.

After two days we reached Kilometre 35, where I was to wait for further orders. The two motorcyclist squads presently caught up with me and we settled in as best we could. We were to stay here for six months.

Kilometre 35. There was no other way of indicating this point, situated thirty-five kilometres from Savannakhet, a little town in Lower Laos on the banks of the Mekong which formed the frontier with Siam. Most of the troops sent from Annam halted here, on the edge of a zone demilitarised in accordance with some old agreement. We were a few hundred yards from a large field which sometimes served as an emergency landing ground for the Air France planes and which was soon to be used by a few Potez 25s and half a dozen Moranes, representing half the fighter aircraft in Indo-China. A battalion of Moi riflemen arrived a few days later, on foot, and was quartered in the same region.

The countryside was flat. This was the 'glade forest' of Laos, consisting of stunted and fairly thinly scattered little

trees through which it was easy to move, unlike the jungle or
forest of Annam.

While waiting for the Siamese, today known as the Thais,
to make up their minds to attack us or—which seemed
more likely to me—for us to attack the Siamese, we encamped
as comfortably as possible in some bamboo huts which the
Laotians from a neighbouring village built for us in a few
days. Time passed quickly at first, divided between establishment duties, a few bouts of malaria and some hunting trips.

The wild fowl (which looked rather like our own barnyard
fowl, but with a more colourful plumage, a more tuneful song
and a flight almost like that of a partridge) began to emerge
from the forest and to gather in 'roosts', as they were called
locally, in the little Laotian paddy fields bordering the tracks.
The time had come to have a go at them by car. They would
rise only at the very last moment, and shooting them on the
wing, while balancing on the back of the seat without stopping
the vehicle, was a beguiling pastime.

The first rains fell and thin grass began to sprout between
the trees in the glade forest. Deer and roebuck swarmed over
the plain. At night their eyes glowed like embers in the beam of
a flashlight probing through the undergrowth. They were an
easy target, of which the English gentlemen of Malaya would
have disapproved. I started by indignantly dismissing the very
idea of such 'sport' but finally yielded, hypocritically saying
to myself that a stag represented food for the whole detachment.

There were also green pigeons and a few ring-doves, which
would fly over our camp at sunset. There were grey part-
ridges whose song, every morning on the edge of the paddy
fields, reminded me forcibly of the hills of Provence . . . Yes,
all things considered, life wasn't so bad in Laos.

We also did a certain amount of military training, though
rather half-heartedly. War with Siam appeared more and
more unlikely.

I did see a few Siamese all the same: far off, through bino-
culars. I had gone to Savannakhet to replenish our supply of

beer and various other drinks. I saw some Siamese on the opposite bank of the Mekong, almost a mile away. They resembled the Laotians on our side like brothers. In fact, they were brothers. Most of the inhabitants of both banks, Thais to a man irrespective of their nationality, were inter-related. The tension, which manifested itself in invective on the wireless and an exchange of notes at a high level, did not appear to have much effect on the people of the Mekong. Every day sampans crossed the river, which made me think there wasn't much the Siamese didn't know about what was going on over on our side.

The local Laotians, however, appeared to view our arrival with a sympathetic eye. They were gentle and hospitable by nature. But if they had seen Siamese troops advancing, I think they would have welcomed them with the same affability. We now knew all the villages in the neighbourhood, where we sometimes went to buy beef or pork. They were all built on the same model, bamboo huts on piles, tucked away in a coconut forest and surrounded by little fields of rice or maize. A few herds of buffalo could be seen moving off to pasture in the glade forest. The women and girls spent all day pounding rice. The men would occasionally go out and do some ploughing, not very energetically. They preferred to wander down to the river and lay a net or snooze in the shade of the coconut trees.

As soon as we arrived, the boys would shin up the trees and shake down a shower of nuts which the young girls then came and offered us, brave warriors that we were, after throwing a shawl round their bare breasts at a discreet sign from the village headman . . . Yes, those were the days!

At the end of the month a martial step was taken by the Government of Indo-China. As a result apparently of further Siamese provocations, we received orders to occupy the demilitarised zone at Kilometre 35 on the Mekong. The A.M.D., still acting as vanguard, moved off towards the river, followed from afar by an infantry battalion.

Thus I arrived one morning at Savannakhet with my four resoled armoured cars and the thirty-two vehicles of the motorcyclist squads. We had received instructions (Top Secret) to make as much of a shindy as possible. Never was an order more punctiliously carried out. We entered the town in a deafening roar of engines. We kept well spaced out and drove at full speed through the streets and along the banks of the Mekong, making a point of going through the same streets several times, following a carefully pre-arranged itinerary, racing round in a crazy circle until the head of the column caught up with the tail, giving the bewildered Laotians and any possible spies the impression that four Panzer divisions were about to break into Thailand: which was the object of the exercise.

After kicking up a great din and raising a monstrous cloud of dust in the quiet streets normally used by placid, domestic buffaloes, we moved off and took up a position along the river, ostentatiously training our machine-guns and rifles on the opposite bank. I couldn't help thinking of Giraudoux's *Trojan War* and of old Demekos racking his brains for insults. Waving my pistol in the direction of the Thailand bank, I yelled, 'O Siamese blockhead ... you're a coward ... your breath stinks ...' But the Thais didn't answer back.

With our armoured cars forming a blockhouse, we spent two days and two nights on the river bank, while the infantry battalion encamped at Savannakhet and started digging in. In a short time the peaceful Laotian city was disfigured by trenches and anti-aircraft shelters. Its mission fulfilled, the A.M.D. then returned to Kilometre 35.

November, 1940

The tension apparently continued. Various incidents were reported on the Cambodian frontier and the Siamese inveighed against us every evening on the wireless; but peace reigned at Kilometre 35. With nothing to occupy them and devoured by malaria, our native soldiers began to show signs of restlessness.

They would buy cheap rice spirit and, in defiance of orders, congregate every evening after curfew round an eighteen-litre carboy of this rotgut. After this there were incidents with the native inhabitants. It was always the same: chickens mysteriously disappearing, girls being molested. There was very little unpleasantness, however, with the Laotians; but the camp was gradually infested by a horde of Annamite merchants with their families, who dispensed tainted meat and adulterated alcohol. The soldiers' pay went into these sharks' pockets, and they sometimes turned nasty.

With the Laotians, on the other hand, our soldiers generally got on very well (both had a splendidly childish mentality). There must be many a fine story about the sojourn of the Colonial Army in this part of Laos. I can only remember one. It happened to one of my men in the A.M.D., a good lad but a terror when he had had one too many. Such was the case on this particular night, when he was prowling round the slumbering village with a couple of pals bent like himself on mischief. They stopped outside the only hut in which a light still glimmered and they fancied they heard the sound of female voices. They started hammering at the door to be let in and, when this was done, burst inside, rabid and ready to commit any outrage.

It was a funeral wake. The deceased's body was laid out on a mat, surrounded by his nearest and dearest reciting litanies, while the joss sticks slowly burned to ashes. It was enough to sober up the three soldiers in a flash. They started by sheepishly doffing their caps, then gradually mingled with the congregation. They too knelt down and clasped their hands in the native manner. In the end they spent the rest of the night there, waking the corpse with as much fervour as the villagers themselves, happy perhaps at finding themselves again in a family atmosphere. I believe they spent their last pennies on contributing some fresh joss sticks. Every case of drunkenness, unfortunately, did not have such a happy ending.

December, 1940

Hostilities eventually broke out (on a modest scale). Two Siamese aircraft flew over Savannakhet and dropped some small twenty-kilo bombs. By way of reprisal, our Potezes went off and bombarded one of their towns in bright moonlight. The Siamese came back and raided Savannakhet, again with small bombs. We were sent off to return their fire, still by way of reprisal, that is to say, to take a few pot shots at the right bank of the Mekong.

Two enemy aircraft subsequently appeared over Kilometre 35, loosing off a few bursts of machine-gun fire and dropping a couple of their little gadgets, which caused no damage at all. This became a regular routine: they would come back every two or three days, drop their miniature bombs, circle round once or twice, then disappear in the direction of the glade forest. The following night the Potezes would go and pay them back in the same coin.

At last I was beginning to move about a bit, but without my armoured cars, which were gradually getting more and more dilapidated. On one occasion I accompanied Lieutenant H. and a motorcyclist squad detailed to escort a company of Mois on their way to Thakek to reinforce the town garrison. Thakek was a Laotian town situated on the banks of the Mekong about seventy miles north of Savannakhet. Since I had no specific duties, I travelled like a tourist, with my inseparable shotgun, admiring a far more impressive forest than the one at Kilometre 35. It was an uneventful trip. The Siamese didn't take the risk of crossing the river, nor did we, and the roar of the motorcyclist squads frightened away all the game.

We settled down at Thakek for the night. Towards midnight I heard the sound of an aircraft, then a series of explosions. It was the first night raid I had ever experienced, and it was neither very heavy nor very close. Yet I felt alarmed. What would the inhabitants of London or Berlin have thought of me?

The town major promptly sent for H. and me. He was under the stress of indescribable emotion. 'Get out of here,' he spluttered, 'get out of here at once... Anywhere you like... Back where you came from... but get out of here.' We couldn't get another word out of him. Obviously he was blaming us for this raid—us with our motorcycles, the infernal din of which could be heard miles away, and the clouds of dust they raised. We assembled our men and equipment and evacuated the town in the middle of the night.

On the way back, at sunrise, I shot a magnificent wild peacock which rose up in front of the car. This trophy made me forget my alarm of the previous night.

January, 1941

A monotonous continuation of the daily light bombardments by the Siamese, the light nocturnal reprisals by the Potezes (by day they would have been too easy a target for fighter aircraft) and a few pot shots from one bank of the Mekong to the other. No one had yet ventured to cross the river. Or rather, yes: one of our sergeants had done so, alone, in a sampan, in broad daylight, without asking anyone's permission, after shaving his pate and donning a bonze's robe. He wandered about on the other side disguised like this for a good hour, but didn't see much apart from some coolies digging trenches and shelters—the same duties on which we were ourselves engaged. He came back without mishap.

The A.M.D. was fairly active for a change. But the programme imposed on us, which was always the same, was not particularly thrilling: we would arrive at night on the banks of the river, in a Laotian village which had been bombarded a few days before. In the dark we would set up all the automatic weapons in the detachment. At first light we would search for military targets on the opposite bank. Since we never found any, we would then carry out the usual reprisals by firing on some abandoned houses, some sampans anchored at the water's edge or some thickets which might possibly conceal trenches. Once the firing was over, we bravely took to our heels without waiting for the Siamese reprisals, which were generally launched several hours later against the peaceful little village in the shape of bombs from aircraft or bursts of machine-gun fire from the enemy bank. This game could go on indefinitely. The only victims were the wretched villagers. We no longer received the hospitable welcome we had enjoyed at first. As soon as they heard the roar of a motorcycle, there would be a general stampede.

February, 1941

There was a rumour that a large-scale attack had been planned in Cambodia, though we received only vague news about it. By way of a diversion, in Laos, on D-day and at zero hour, a violent fusillade by every unit (including several batteries of artillery that had recently arrived) was launched all the way along the Mekong on a front of nearly a hundred miles. The A.M.D. did not take part in this fun-and-games; but from our camp we could hear the sound of the batteries, which lasted several hours. For a country which was short of ammunition, this seemed fantastic. Two assaults were attempted the following night by some Moi companies, but were only partially successful. A number of riflemen and one French sergeant lost their lives.

Then the whole thing died down. There was no more talk of the offensive in Cambodia. We heard on the wireless of a brilliant victory won by the Indo-Chinese Navy over the Siamese Navy. A wag in the A.M.D. pointed out that there was no Indo-Chinese Navy. There was no Siamese Navy either. But the former had sunk the latter in a battle which would go down in history.

March, 1941

Total inactivity, barely punctuated by one or two air raid alarms. The Siamese now hardly ever came and flew over us.

They had one success, however: a couple of Moranes destroyed on the ground, on the air-field; in other words, twenty per cent of the Indo-Chinese fighter aircraft.

This looked like the end. Morale was low. I spent every afternoon creeping through the trees in the glade forest, trying to stalk the herds of deer which our warlike demonstrations had unnerved.

There was a rumour that the end of hostilities was imminent. In point of fact, the Japanese, who had been pulling the strings since the start of the incident, had found the moment favourable to appear in the light of mediators and were seizing this opportunity to establish themselves in strength in Cochin-China.

April, 1941

It was soon over. A sort of armistice was signed. I believe we gave the Thais more or less all they demanded, but no one seemed to know exactly what it was all about. We went back to Hué and decorations were distributed to the officers who had taken part in the campaign.

I had started drawing up plans again, more precise plans this time, to get back to British territory, when, to my great surprise, a circular from the Governor General decreed the demobilisation and repatriation of every Frenchman who had come from abroad. I was once more full of hope and well-being after this long period of discouragement. I said good-bye to my friends and went down to Saigon, hoping to take ship as soon as possible for Singapore.

May, 1941

In Saigon I came across other friends from Malaya, demobilised like myself, who had been through various adventures here. The only absentee was Barbier, who had not waited for official permission but had left Indo-China on board a Potez shortly after the armistice. We drank to our departure which we considered imminent. We were in order with the French authorities. All that remained was to get permission from the British to enter Singapore: a mere formality, we imagined. We went in a body to the consul to obtain the necessary visa. He replied that he couldn't give it to us at once but would have to refer the matter to Singapore. We were to wait for this visa for another three months!

June, 1941

Waiting in Saigon became more and more of a strain. Impossible to get the British visa. Always the same reply at the consulate, where we called twice a day: 'Wait.' Distrust? Administrative slackness? I never discovered. When some of us asked point blank: 'If we manage to get to Malaya without proper papers, for the purpose of joining Free France, what will happen to us?' the vice-consul replied: 'You're bound to be sent back here to Indo-China.' Yet at this very moment the French papers were all saying that the British were recruiting foreign mercenaries by every possible means, from promises to intimidation!

At the Hotel Continental, where we were staying, the Malayans' table became more and more despondent.

I ran into an old school friend, a naval officer, who invited me to dine on shipboard. He told me with unconcealed pride that he had taken part in an expedition aimed at the reconquest of New Caledonia (which joined Free France on the first day). The attempt did not succeeed, he said, because of two British cruisers patrolling in the vicinity. It was obvious that he bitterly regretted not having sunk one of these vessels. I did my best to remain impassive and refused to discuss the question. At this time one had to weigh one's words carefully in Saigon, even in front of old friends. The local press reported the German successes in progressively sickening terms—even worse, I believe, than the worst collaborationist press in France.

Japanese in civilian clothes began to make an appearance here and there and a section of the Hotel Continental was reserved for them. There was an economic mission and also the mission for the delimitation of the frontier with Siam. There was every type among them, from the extremely diffident with gentlemanly manners to the flashy bounder who thought it good taste to walk around in his shorts and sock garters, just to show that nothing appertaining to civilisation was alien to him. There was the Jap who lived on a handful of rice and water and there was the Jap who started off the day by drinking a bottle of whisky to whet his appetite, knocked off a bottle of gin on top of that and then bellowed for a bottle of brandy.

Things were going rather badly in Europe; the Russians seemed to be caving in. The Greeks were being crushed by the German armoured columns. Wavell, after a brilliant campaign, was in retreat and had yielded part of the territory conquered from the Italians in Africa. There was a red-letter day, however, after a series of bad news. While we were sitting on the terrace of the Continental, the manager came up and whispered in our ear that the *Bismarck* had been sunk. At the Malayans' table we drank exuberantly to this item of good news. Seated at the next table was a tall fellow guest who looked mortified and darted furious glances at us. He was the new German consul in Saigon.

July, 1941

I went off to Cap Saint-Jacques for a few days. If this situation went on much longer, I would end up by knowing this country better than Malaya. On my return there were two important incidents, the one important to Indo-China, the other to myself.

The first was the landing of a Japanese army in Cochin-China with the agreement and blessing of the Government General. A Franco-Japanese gala was organised in Saigon.

The second was, at last, the long-awaited permission to go back to Malaya (I had a feeling it had come just in time). But the latter made me almost forget the former. After two years spent in Indo-China, where I thought I would be staying no more than one month, I embarked for Singapore feeling almost light-hearted, so eager was I to escape this painful atmosphere of resignation and defeatism.

From Malaya to China

I

SINGAPORE 1941

August, 1941

We arrived at Singapore along with some Englishmen from Indo-China who were anxious to avoid contact with the Japanese. I rejoined de Langlade and my planter friends, both English and French. If at this stage I entertained a slight doubt as to what line of conduct to follow, five minutes' conversation with de Langlade dispelled it and I signed my enlistment in Free France a few days after my arrival.

Here I must apologise, in a narrative dealing above all with facts and adventures, for indulging in a short digression aimed at examining as closely as possible a state of mind (mine) —a difficult task, a sometimes fascinating and frequently tedious task, which in the present case ends in total failure. It is not without reason that I have used this conjectural turn of phrase: 'If at this stage I entertained a slight doubt...' It would perhaps be more glorious to depict my enlistment as the result of a firm intention ever since the 18th of June. I have already hinted that this was not the case: I have spoken of temptations, vague urges, indecision. Moreover, harassed by the memory of this indecision, I might perhaps be sorely tempted (a sort of masochism much more common than is generally believed) to blacken myself deliberately by exaggerating it and to depict myself as being influenced only by external circumstances. I don't think this was the case either. What point had I reached exactly when I set foot in Singapore again? What really was my state of mind and the

43

nature of my will? I must confess, with my hand on my heart, that *I don't know at all*. My only certainty is that my decision was taken, and did not alter again afterwards, after five minutes' conversation with de Langlade. Of this, and only this, am I sure.

There is a second delicate and obscure point that worries me, and the novelist that I am today cannot avoid pointing it out; after which I think I shall have finished with my valorous attempts at introspection. It consists in trying to determine in what proportions there entered into this decision patriotism and a sense of duty on the one hand and, on the other, pride and the selfish prospect of experiencing elating and unusual adventures. Alas, here again, *I don't know at all*. It is a question I have often asked myself since. I have never been able to find an answer. I have never managed to solve this problem and I don't think there is much chance that I ever shall.

Be that as it may, my enlistment marked the beginning of a series of adventures which were to have a marked effect on my life, and this may be the only important thing.

The Free French team in Malaya was somewhat thin on the ground (to say the least!). It was mainly made up of the planters from our company, most of whom were still in the rubber fields waiting to be able to play a more active role. At Singapore itself the 'Mission' (two tiny offices in a huge block) consisted of the former Governor of Pondicherry as official representative, Professor May, a surgeon who had fled from pro-Vichy Indo-China, Lieutenant Jacosta, a strange character to whom I shall refer later, who came from heaven knows where, and one or two others. Brizay, who worked as an architect in Singapore and looked after colleagues in transit, came and called on us frequently. In fact I believe the whole organisation hinged on de Langlade who, while retaining his civilian post, divided his time between Kuala Lumpur and Singapore, contributing to the cause of Free France in the Far East his ardour, his natural authority, the authority due to his professional standing, his incomparable gift for man-management and his valuable connections among the British.

An initial problem had cropped up long before my arrival: every member of the little team was firmly resolved to make himself useful, but how? Which was the best way? Should he go to England? Some had already done so. Barbier, after a memorable escape from Indo-China, had pursued his course and was now in London. Léonard was in a training camp in Africa. Others talked of following suit. But de Langlade had other ideas and convinced us that we would be more useful if we stayed here.

His arguments carried weight: he was more or less certain that war was imminent between the Allies and Japan and that South-East Asia would become an important theatre of operations sooner or later. Indo-China, now occupied by the enemy, began to shimmer before our dazzled eyes with a particular glow. The reconquest of Indo-China was surely an obvious ideal for us Frenchmen in Malaya. Indo-China was only two or three days by boat from Singapore, this impregnable fortress which would become, we felt sure, the focal point of the war in the Far East and even of the whole war! Two or three days by boat, scarcely more by submarine, only a few hours by air. We conjured up in our imagination a mysterious world of parachute drops or clandestine landings on deserted beaches, elating dreams which were to last until the fall of Singapore and revive shortly afterwards in different forms.

I learned (which I did not know, although I had just come back) that there were already some small groups over there resolved to continue the struggle, in particular Bocquet and his friends (more rubber planters!). Our original plan, feverishly drawn up, consisted in preparing a fifth column organisation over there, with a view to sabotaging the Japanese installations on the day war was declared against the Allies.

The English said they were ready to help us; at least their clandestine organisations said so, for they were not yet at war

45

with Japan. But this was not the least attraction of the adventure: to collaborate, even in a modest way, with the one and only Intelligence Service! I would have given ten years of my life for this at the time!

The British organisation dealing with enemy installations abroad (subsequently Force 136) invited me to undertake a course at the Convent, a course which other planters had already followed. The Convent was the name given to a very special school situated in the jungle and sheltered from all prying eyes. Solemn gentlemen methodically instructed us there in the art of blowing up a bridge, fixing an explosive charge to the side of a ship, derailing a train and also putting an end to an enemy sentry as silently as possible. This last point seemed to prey on the mind of one of the instructors, as though the technique had not yet been perfected. There were countless demonstrations on dummies, followed by discussions at which each of us was invited to express in logical order the reasons for which he preferred slitting a man's throat with a knife rather than bashing him over the head with a club.

Having finished the course, I worked for some time in an office in Singapore, correlating the intelligence coming in from here and there. I was not particularly happy in this job, especially since de Langlade had meanwhile left for Indo-China, under a false name and with a false passport, to see how the land lay. He was to spend almost a month there without being discovered, which was a bit of luck, for the local Sûreté was aware of his identity. He established some valuable contacts and came back safely, after being fished out of the Baie d'Along by the British clandestine organisation.

September, 1941

Office work began to weigh more and more heavily on me. At last an expedition was planned, in which I was to take part. Professor May, who consorted with the high and mighty, came to brief me about it at the Hotel Adelphi where I was quartered. The briefing was conducted in an atmosphere of mystery which filled me with awe. He walked round the hotel three times before coming into the bar, and sat down at a table only after making sure that no one could hear us.

The plan was as follows: we were to embark on a boat provided by the British and with a Malay crew, arrive after dark off the Indo-Chinese coast, and land about a ton of explosives (this was something to start with) and demolition equipment which were now familiar to me. I was to stay behind in Indo-China under the protection of the planters together with R., another Frenchman, who was a wireless specialist. My duties, as a so-called sabotage expert, would entail instructing a number of young men in the art of demolition.

May was also to take part in the expedition but was due to return to Singapore, together with three British officers who were to accompany us and lend a hand in case of an emergency.

Our departure day duly arrived. To be frank, I must admit that the means put at our disposal by the clandestine organisation did not strike me as being perfectly adapted to the enterprise. I even had a slight shock when I saw the boat which was to take us. It was flat-bottomed and without a keel. In fact, it was a launch which used to ply the Shanghai River; that is to say that any French or Japanese sailor would consider it suspicious if he observed it at sea. I thought of the past masters of espionage who spent weeks attending to the smallest details of their disguise, of the secret agents who lived for years in India, Malaya and the Philippines, managing to pass themselves off as natives. Maybe there was no other boat available. But there was no getting away from it; this boat, loaded with explosives and selected to pass unnoticed on enemy seas, was a river launch. The three British officers discussed this choice with their customary humour.

We loaded the explosives and equipment, which were concealed in huge suitcases, and sailed from Singapore one fine morning, escorted through the minefields by some units of the Royal Navy.

The first two days at sea were uneventful, apart from our all lying prostrate in our bunks, overcome by sea-sickness. This keelless boat pitched and rolled and shook us up unmercifully. Even the Malay crew were seasick.

On the third day we received a signal from Singapore which no one was able to decipher. One of the joys of clandestine messages at this stage was that very few people, even in possession of the code, were able to understand them. We asked for a repeat. Meanwhile, to while away the time and try to forget our sea-sickness, the Anglo-French team got down to work, trying every possible combination in an attempt to make some sense of the mysterious series of letters forming words that looked like Polish or Serbo-Croat. It was not until the following day that we discovered the solution, after deductions which Dupin and Sherlock Holmes would have admired. (The signal had meanwhile been repeated but was still indecipherable.) It was high time; the message ran more or less as follows: 'Indo-China alerted. Japanese keeping close watch on rendezvous point. Return immediately.' We were then not very far from the coast and, as we learned later, a Japanese squadron was cruising in the vicinity.

We turned about and sailed back to Singapore, not very proud of this initial setback which was to be followed by several more.

October, 1941

While the authorities were preparing a fresh expedition, I resumed my office work, which bored me more and more. Even the company of the strange character who ran this office didn't succeed in reconciling me to the the monotony.

Jacosta was a French lieutenant who had come from Indo-China. At least that was what he said on arriving here. He spoke English, German, Russian, Czech and several Middle Eastern dialects. This was no empty boast; one day I heard him interrogate some Foreign Legion soldiers of various nationalities who were passing through Singapore, each one in his own language. According to his own statements, he had lived a long time in Russia, then in the East, where he worked with the French Deuxième Bureau. Still according to him, he had been in Spain during the Civil War and had commanded a Communist division. He claimed to have been the secretary of the G.O.C. Indo-China. Yet no one there appeared to have known him. Perhaps, however, the British had more detailed information on his previous career, for they seemed to trust him completely. His accent occasionally had a foreign intonation. Tall, lean, ascetic-looking, living alone, interested apparently in nothing but his work, he struck me as being a really professional Intelligence officer. He showed extraordinary patience and activity in this field, using methods which shocked me in spite of myself, spying on friend as well as foe. He worked fifteen hours a day and had had a camp bed installed in the office, where he would sometimes spend the night.

He left us at the end of October, on a mission to Shanghai and Hong Kong. I never saw him again. I have since heard that at the time of the fall of Hong Kong, he volunteered to ensure the defense of a power station with a handful of friends. While he was outside the station for a few minutes, some shots were heard. He didn't come back and his body was never found. The enigma of Jacosta has never been solved as far as I know.

November, 1941

The news emanating from Japan was bad. Here, however, no one seemed to believe in war. Life in Singapore was as gay as ever. Every evening, on the terrace of Raffles, the khaki uniforms of the Indian Army and the white jackets of the naval officers rubbed shoulders with the dinner jackets of the civilians. In the night clubs, the taxi girls (Chinese, Siamese, Malays, Eurasians) had never seen so many customers. The Japanese colony, which included almost all the photographers, barbers and night-club proprietors, impassively eavesdropped every day on the conversation exchanged by the whiskered officers.

Yet the British and American papers were full of threats and warnings concerning the Japanese Empire. America had only just stopped its supplies of oil, and the fashionable slogan was the ABCD (American-British-Chinese-Dutch) encirclement of Japan. Every day the local press announced that fresh reinforcements had reached Singapore. We were all convinced that Malaya was now defended by an army of three hundred thousand men and a thousand modern aircraft.

A Japanese delegation had gone to America to protest against the ABCD encirclement, and discussions were under way.

December, 1941

While the U.S. State Department conferred with Japanese envoys, while the American fleet slumbered in Pearl Harbour, while the military command in Malaya, so as not to alarm the inhabitants, stopped requisitioning several thousand coolies needed for the construction of some elementary defense works, while the gentlemen of Hong Kong refused to dig trenches on the golf course, which would have disfigured it, while General Chiang Kai-shek and his wife observed with a hopeful eye the mounting tension in Nippo-American relations, while the Governor General of French Indo-China received the decoration of the Grand Rising Sun, while Europe, having other fish to fry, turned her eyes away from the Far East, the Japanese at zero hour embarked on a programme they had been planning in detail for months and launched an attack against the Pacific Isles, Malaya and the British possessions in China.

I was wakened at three in the morning by the sound of explosions. I got up and looked out of the window. The streets of Singapore were empty and illuminated in the normal way. Convinced it must be a night exercise, I peacefully went back to sleep. Next morning, on my way to the office, I learned from the papers that we were at war with Japan and that America had entered the lists. I went and had a look at the damage caused by the first bombs, which had fallen on Raffles Square. The onlookers were discussing the latest news, which was anything but good but still did not tally with the actual facts. It appeared that during the night the Japanese had inflicted serious damage on the American fleet, that they had landed in the Philippines and, above all, in Malaya itself, in the Kra Isthmus.

I rushed round to the office, which was now run by Major T., who had been sent out from London as head of the Free French Military Mission. He had arrived two days before at the same time as Léonard, one of our planters, who on mobilisation had spent some time in Africa and then been posted back here where it was considered he might be more useful.

T. maintained his composure, whereas we were all inclined to lose ours. He went on methodically filing his notes and cards, like the professional Intelligence officer that he too was. He had arrived in Singapore with the firm intention, I believe, of installing the mission in China. The latest events merely confirmed his determination and he calmly continued to work on this project. He was no doubt right, and I was wrong to be exasperated by his impassivity.

But the shock of the Japanese invasion had another result for us. De Langlade arrived a few days later, having completely abandoned his civilian duties to devote himself to the service of Free France. A fresh dynamism seized the mission. De Langlade obviously shared our point of view: we had to try to do something, at once.

Do something, at once, but what? It was not difficult for our feverish minds to imagine. He wrote an official letter to the Commander-in-Chief, Malaya. I have forgotten the exact text, but it ran more or less as follows: 'We are a small group of Frenchmen here whose one desire is to collaborate with you. It is now some months since we suggested to you the organisation of a fifth column in Indo-China. So far your help has

been meagre and the relations you entertain with the representatives of the Vichy Government upset our plans. In point of
fact, the Japanese have used Indo-China as a spring-board for
their aggression, and the usefulness of a fifth column over there
at this moment is obvious. We ask you now to provide us with
an aircraft and equipment for the immediate parachuting into
Indo-China of two Frenchmen [de Langlade and myself]
who will try to organise sabotage commandos.'

This proposal impressed the C.-in-C., who was all in favour
of the plan, and we started preparing our equipment in an
atmosphere of unimaginable over-excitement. Alas, a few days
later, and after several conferences between the heads of the
various departments concerned, this plan proved to be impracticable: out of the four planes capable of making the flight
there and back, two had already been shot down and the
remaining two were considered too valuable to risk on a
mission of this sort.

Besides, the war in the Far East now began to assume an
altogether different aspect. It was soon obvious that neither
Malaya nor Hong Kong nor the Philippines would be able to
hold out. Burma and the Dutch East Indies would probably
fall in their turn. This war was going to last a long time and a
lot of ground would have to be yielded.

Setback followed setback. In Malaya the Japanese seized
Penang after two weeks' fighting and were now marching
against Kuala Lumpur. Hong Kong was being besieged and its
fall was only a question of days. MacArthur, for all his
exploits, had to abandon the Philippines. Finally—a day of
mourning for England and for all of us—two capital ships, the
Prince of Wales and the *Repulse*, were sunk by Japanese aircraft (based on Indo-China, alas!). The *Prince of Wales* was
one of the finest units in the Navy. Furthermore, she was a
historic vessel: Churchill and Roosevelt had met on board.
She was the first modern battleship the English had lost. She
had been dispatched to the disembarkation point in the hope
that her firepower might cause havoc among the enemy ship-

ping, but without a fighter plane to protect her. She sank in a few minutes without being able to use a single one of her huge guns.

I heard the bombardment from Singapore itself. The next evening all the night clubs were invaded by the sailors who had survived the disaster. They looked less dejected than anyone else and gave a spirited account of the sinking, describing how the admiral in command had asked for his dress cap before going down with his ship in the China Seas.

De Langlade and Major T. were now agreed on transferring the mission to China, probably to Kunming (or Yunnanfu), the capital of Yunnan. We were all to move up there by way of Rangoon. This was some consolation to me. I had missed being parachuted into Indo-China, but at least I should get to know the famous road, the name of which—I don't know why—had been haunting me for ages: the Burma Road, the Road to Mandalay.

Our departures were staggered. T. was the first to leave. He was to stop off in Rangoon and contact d'Iribarne (another of our planters), who had been stationed there for a month. De Langlade was to leave four days afterwards, I, a week later, and Léonard just before the fall of Singapore. We were to travel in civilian clothes, under false names, of course, and with British passports. Why? In the first place, no one at this juncture would be so rash as to travel along the Burma Road and, above all, enter China under his real identity. This simply wasn't done in the hush-hush organisation with which we were collaborating. Secondly, it was a necessity for us Frenchmen, so as to avoid complications with the Chinese and Chiang Kai-shek, who took their cue from America and still refused to recognise Free France. So I became P. J. Rule, born in Mauritius, a British subject; de Langlade was quite simply Long. The famous organisation had asked us to choose our names ourselves before issuing our passports. We didn't rack our brains over the choice.

January, 1942

I spent the evening of January 1 in the restaurant of the Cathay, the Singapore skyscraper. People went on carousing there in spite of the Japanese advance, and without bothering unduly about the increasingly more frequent air raid alarms. The only difference was the temperature. The oxygen of the air-conditioning system had been requisitioned by the army and a torrid heat reigned in the building with its blacked-out windows.

Outside, in the equatorial dark, searchlights scanned the skies above Singapore harbour for enemy aircraft. This seemed to be the only efficient branch of the service. They almost always succeeded in spotting the planes and then hung on to them. The targets could easily be seen with the naked eye, like brighter stars in the unbroken shaft of light. The anti-aircraft guns would sprinkle the sky with red dots, which the aircraft seemed scarcely to notice. Most people in the Cathay went on dancing during the raids. The British lion refused to be roused by these pin-pricks and there had not yet been a particularly heavy bombardment.

After de Langlade's departure I in my turn packed my bags. Since I was entitled to 25 pounds only, my packing consisted of destroying everything else or giving it away to the hotel boys.

One last tour in Malaya, a final farewell to the plantations; with Léonard I made a flying visit to Kuala Lumpur. We travelled by car and throughout the three-hundred-mile drive we saw not a single soldier, road-block or control point. In an almost deserted Kuala Lumpur we called on J. Nicol, the new director of our company since de Langlade had resigned the position. He was getting ready to move off at short notice, taking the company archives with him in a huge trunk. We spent the evening reminiscing over the past, then dossed down in his bungalow. The Japanese were no more than a few miles north of the town. Gunfire could be heard fairly close, but it was not very heavy. We drove off next morning after bidding our host a tender farewell. On the way back we passed a num-

'ber of British troops withdrawing southwards. We saw one makeshift barricade on the road, made of old petrol tins. In spite of our French uniforms and unfamiliar badges of rank, we drove along unmolested. No one asked to see our papers and we were not stopped once.

At Singapore the evacuation of the women and children had started. Ships, filled to capacity, were detailed to take them to India, Australia or the Dutch East Indies, from which the refugees were due to move again a few weeks later in similar conditions. All of them were leaving behind precious possessions accumulated over the years they had spent here. In general they showed great fortitude.

The hour of departure at last rang for me. Under the name of P. J. Rule, taking with me three or four pairs of shorts, the same number of shirts, the somewhat shabby suit in which I had arrived in Malaya five years before (it was said to be cold in Kunming), a revolver (of very small calibre: that was all the organisation could find for me), a compass and a few maps, I embarked on a flying boat which was to take me first to Rangoon. I left my car at the gates of the airport, with the ignition key in the dashboard.

THE BURMA ROAD

January, 1942

It was normally only a few hours' flight from Singapore to Rangoon, but the Japanese fighters did not allow us to follow a straight course and it took me four days to reach Burma. On taking off, the flying boat headed due south, whereas Rangoon lay to the north, but no one on board showed the slightest surprise. We flew over some islands in the Malay Archipelago, skirted the southernmost tip of Sumatra and touched down in the afternoon at Batavia.

We spent the night in the Javanese capital, quartered in a sumptuous Dutch hotel. The passengers on the flying boat were almost all British officers in mufti engaged on more or less mysterious activities. I already knew some of them, but we pretended to be meeting for the first time. No one asked any questions.

We took off again at dawn, this time heading north-west, and flew all the way along the west coast of Sumatra. This was one of the loveliest flights I had known. The Dutch East Indies were much more colourful than Malaya. The sky here was clearer, the sea more blue. The palm trees in the plantations had a golden glint which I had never seen anywhere else.

We touched down early in the afternoon near the northern tip of Sumatra. We were not allowed to go ashore and spent the night in a small cargo ship lying at anchor.

On the third day we crossed the Bay of Bengal. After flying over countless little islands which make up the Nicobar Archipelago, we touched down in the Andamans, at Port Blair. The island, which used to serve as a penitentiary, had been evacuated, with the exception of two or three Indian bearers who were on duty in the hotel. At last, on the fourth day, we arrived at Rangoon, after reaching the coast well to the west, flying over the vast expanse of paddy fields forming Lower Burma, and then coming back to the port.

Rangoon. Dazzling gold pagodas rose above the dirty town, where garbage disposal was mostly left to the rooks and scavengers. Just as in Malaya one saw hardly any Malays, so in Burma Burmans were few and far between, at least in the towns. On the other hand, one came across Indians from every part of India. The most current language was Hindustani.

The town had been severely bombarded. Some of the native population had taken refuge in the outskirts and dozens of corpses still lay in the streets as a result of the disorganisation of the public services. There were still air raid warnings, but the corps of American volunteers to China, Colonel Chennault's Flying Tigers, had recently established a base in Rangoon and the Japanese air force was suffering heavy losses.

I found Major T. and d'Iribarne quartered in the only hotel which was still open. De Langlade, or rather Long (I shall call him this from now on), had already left for Kunming, driving a British truck. T. was to leave on the evening of my arrival, by train as far as Mandalay, then by plane to Chungking, where he hoped to meet General Chiang Kai-shek. I wanted to move on straight away, but T. asked me to wait here until he sent me word, the Chinese apparently having not yet agreed to our being allowed into China even under false names and with British passports.

So I stayed on in Rangoon with d'Iribarne. We went sight-seeing in the town, which would have been pleasant had it not been so dirty. It was the cool season. The atmosphere was clear and bright, with an occasional nip in the air to which I was unaccustomed after my years in Malaya and Indo-China. We wandered round the pagodas whose glorious golden domes rose above an incredible labyrinth of hovels and corrugated-iron shacks. In the evening we dined at the only restaurant which had kept its doors open. It was patronised by all the civilian and military organisations dealing with the traffic on the Burma Road, and God knows how many there were! The Americans and British were not always on good terms and scuffles occasionally occurred. It was a far cry from the elegant, formal environment of Singapore, and the very opposite of a gentleman's club. The Burma Road had attracted quite a number of adventurers and the police were more or less non-existent. Inside the restaurant their duties were performed by the proprietors, two Armenian brothers, ex-pugilists, who had been stranded here for some reason or other but were now busy making a fortune and more or less kept law and order. All this made a pleasantly colourful picture, but I couldn't stop thinking of the Burma Road and the picture soon palled.

A signal from T. at last informed me that I was able to enter China, which I believe I could have done much earlier. D'Iribarne was to stay on here a little longer. I now merely had to find a means of transport. I could always fly, of course, but it was the Road that attracted me. On the off chance, I called at one of the British offices. A stroke of luck: they had just requisitioned an almost new Buick intended for the British Consul at Kunming, and were looking for someone to drive it up there. I pounced on this miraculous opportunity. I took charge of the car. I barely spared the time to say good-bye to d'Iribarne, for fear of a counter-order. I even forgot to ask him for some money, for he was in charge of the funds. I overlooked the visa formalities and, towards two in the afternoon, started off along the Burma Road.

On January 30, 1942, equipped with a brand-new British passport and afflicted with an accent which betrayed him as a native of the Vaucluse, without any valid papers, without even having enough money (an indispensable safe-conduct in China), Peter John Rule, born in Mauritius and British by birth through the machinations of the British and Chinese

58

secret services combined, following in the wake of numerous American convoys towards Mandalay, towards China, almost towards Tibet and the Himalayas, sallied forth on the conquest of Indo-China with a miniature revolver in his pocket and at the wheel of a motor car which would not have been out of place on the Riviera. The memory of that moment was to console me for many a subsequent disappointment.

February, 1942

Come you back, you British soldier;
come you back to Mandalay!

Rangoon, Pegu, Toungoo ... I drove all the way across lower Burma, about two hundred and fifty miles of flat roads, without even sparing a glance for the countryside, so great was my impatience to reach the mountains. My only memory is of buffalo carts forming an uninterrupted column along the tracks reserved for them on either side of the road. The vehicles were laden with Burmans in multi-coloured sarongs, most of them fast asleep, including the driver.

Before leaving, I had decided to drive in one lap into China. I had not thought of the petrol problem. Petrol stations were few and far between on the Burma Road; at night they were closed. I prudently stopped in a deserted spot, which I calculated to be about forty miles from Mandalay. I spent the night in the car, wakened from time to time by the noise of a convoy of lorries.

I started off again early in the morning and reached Mandalay just as the golden pagodas were beginning to sparkle in the rising sun. I found some petrol fairly easily and, without lingering to look at the palace of the Burman emperors, at last climbed out of the plain and into the mountains, which I was not to leave again for some time.

The first impression of the Road was extraordinary—even

better than I had imagined. I stopped a few miles above Mandalay, which was dominated by sheer cliffs bathed in a marvellous light. In the distance I could see the immensity of the Burma Plain, with its green paddy fields bordering the Irrawaddy. The huge South-Asiatic range started abruptly at my feet and extended above my head into other loftier, more chaotic, more mysterious mountains. No film has ever given an idea of this landscape. Nothing here resembled what I had seen in Malaya or Indo-China. The sky was bluer than the sky of Annam; the air was as sparkling as the air of Provence in spring; and the forest, which was as thick as the Malay jungle, did not exude the smell of decay characteristic of equatorial flora.

Mandalay lay at my feet: Mandalay, the town with pagodas even more dazzling than those of Rangoon; Mandalay, with its palace which housed generations of Oriental despots famous for their quarrels and the murders in which they all indulged, so much so that one day the British lion decided to come and establish a little order among them; Mandalay, whose conquest by the handsome soldiers of the Indian Army was hymned by Kipling* and which was presently to experience the Japanese invasion. The few unfortunate thousands of British soldiers defending Rangoon and the plain were soon to be driven back towards these cliffs, cross these reputedly impassable mountains, make their way to India and from there prepare for a glorious return.

I bathed in a waterfall streaming down towards the plain, then continued my ascent towards China. The next stop was Lashio, the last big town in Burma. I arrived there at nightfall, after having driven about six hundred miles. From Mandalay to Lashio I crossed the Shan States, the wildest part of Burma. The few natives I passed looked like hardy mountainfolk and bore no resemblance to the rather effeminate Burmans of the plain.

Lashio lies at an altitude of over three thousand five hun-

* Kipling again—what dreadful colonialists we were!

dred feet and as soon as I reached it I had a sensation of icy cold. Where were the stifling nights of Singapore? I lay down on a camp bed in a British Army transport camp and, even with two blankets over me, I shivered. A dormant germ of malaria had been revived. I intended leaving again early next morning, but the Buick was in no fit state. I had probably knocked it about a bit on the winding roads above Mandalay. Fortunately a repairs workshop took charge of it. I seized this opportunity to visit the town.

In the old days there had been nothing remarkable about it. It was the Burma Road that gave it its present importance. Americans, English and Chinese had turned it into a supplies centre and a large part of the equipment destined for China was stored here. It housed not only the military and civilian transport services, but also a host of merchants, racketeers, smugglers, adventurers, anyone who owned a truck or even a horse-drawn vehicle, Chinese, Indians, Burmans and also Europeans whom the attraction of the Road and its traffic had brought to this corner of Asia. It was not only arms and ammunition for the regular troops that passed along the Burma road!

At noon my car was ready. I said good-bye to the Englishmen who had put me up, telling them of my intention to drive all day and night so as to reach Kunming the following morning. This brought a smile to the lips of one of them who knew both the Road and China, especially when I mentioned that I had no valid papers for the car and didn't speak a word of Chinese. According to him, it would take me at least eight days, even assuming I got there, which was far from certain. He took pity on the young madman that I was and scribbled a few Chinese characters on a card for me. With this, he explained, I might have some hope of getting petrol, which was said to be even more of a problem than in Burma.

I left Lashio and headed for the frontier, which I reached after dark. I was lucky enough to be able to fill up for the last time in Burma.

61

I drove through the first barrier, the British frontier, after a five-minute session with an official. It was ten o'clock at night when I drew up at the Chinese barricade. There my difficulties began.

There were two separate administrations, one civilian, the other military, which vied with each other, as far as I could see, as to which should obtain the biggest bribe in a case like mine. I spent a large part of the night going from one to the other, trying to convince them that P. J. Rule was neither a smuggler nor a spy. After all, I had a letter from an official in Rangoon, which should facilitate the formalities for me. The civilian Customs men were eventually wheedled into allowing me to pass through, but not without making me pay a toll of two thousand Chinese dollars for my car. (It was not a huge sum, but it was too much for me at the moment.) The military refused to play and I was not rich enough to use the same irresistible argument with them. I felt sure, however, from the garbled explanations of a Chinese in spectacles who had benevolently offered to act as an interpreter, that a generous gesture on my part would arrange everything, but this was beyond my means.

After a lengthy discussion, I had a brain wave. I went and sat in the car on the side of the road, facing the barrier, and with a smile announced that I wouldn't budge from there. I had, I believe, taken the only reasonable line in China when everything goes badly: to wait, albeit without showing the slightest impatience. This didn't have an immediate effect. The lieutenant in command of the post merely went back to bed and no one seemed to pay any more attention to me. I dozed until daybreak, wakened every now and then by figures prowling silently round the car. I didn't feel safe, in spite of the proximity of the guard post, and kept a special watch on the petrol tank.

In the morning the post paraded on the side of the road and, in the first beams of the rising sun, I saw the Chinese flag hoisted for the first time while the soldiers sang the national anthem in raucous voices. It was a pretty impressive ceremony in these surroundings and it was not at all from a spirit of mockery that I stood stiffly to attention until the end, wondering all the same how many more times I would see this flag hoisted before being able to continue on my journey. But suddenly, moved perhaps by this demonstration of sympathy, or more probably tired of seeing me still there and satisfied (or humiliated) to realise that I was as patient as himself, the lieutenant suddenly walked up, raised the barrier himself and with an air of disgust motioned me to drive through. I entered China, inwardly extremely proud of having got the better of him.

I tried to make up for the time I had wasted and drove as fast as the state of the narrow, winding road and the convoys of trucks that had started off after the night's halt permitted. Between Wantung, the frontier village, and Kunming there was an almost continuous stream of traffic in both directions. Time and again I felt sure that the consul in Kunming would never see the Buick intended for him, especially since the Burma Road seemed to have a particular highway code of its own. In Malaya you drive on the left; in Indo-China on the right. On the Road no one, least of all the Chinese, recognised left or right; everyone drove without hesitation on the side nearest the mountain, leaving the edge of the precipice to the wretches unaccustomed to such thoroughfares. Furthermore, they would switch off their engines at the top of each hill and coast down the long slopes in neutral so as to be able to sell on the black market the few drops of petrol they had thereby saved. This, even more than the air raids, I believe, accounted for the number of gutted trucks lying at the bottom of the ravines. Their cargo had been looted straight away.

The Burma Road was frequently enveloped in an almost opaque cloud of choking, ochre-coloured dust—which was a pity, for what I was able to see through the intervening gaps revealed one of the loveliest landscapes in South-East Asia. It was an endless succession of precipices, peaks, saddles, smiling valleys, and waterfalls which, with their variety, quaintness and grandiose proportions, would no doubt one day turn this road into a world-renowned tourist route.*

If only I had had time to spend a few days on the banks of the Salween! It was the first river in China that I crossed (on a bridge destroyed time and again by bombing and time and again rebuilt a few hours afterwards by the Chinese). At its mouth, in the Gulf of Martaban, it is several miles across and dyed the colour of mud as a result of flowing through the plain. But here it was no more than forty yards wide and the water was as clear as an Alpine stream. The road ran alongside it for several miles before crossing it. I stopped for a few minutes to get out of range of the trucks and the dust, and contemplated an admirable valley sweeping down from a prodigious mass of mountains varying in tone all the way to the horizon, beyond which I pictured the mysterious land of Tibet.

I took to the road again with regret. But it was not to admire the blue mountains or to dream about Lhasa that P. J. Rule was at the wheel of a Buick on the roads of China. His purpose was to reach Kunming. After the toll paid to the sharks on the frontier, I reckoned I had just enough dollars left to buy the petrol I needed, and then only provided I could find a moderately black market. I had had nothing to eat since Lashio. I resolved to continue my fast until I arrived. That would mean three days without food.

After the Salween Valley I drove through Paoshan, a little town surrounded by ramparts, which was soon to become a big operations centre. It was between the Salween and Paoshan that the Japanese, after the conquest of Burma, were halted after their thrust towards Yunnan. No one would ever know if this was due to the Chinese armies or the mountains. Further on I crossed the Mekong, on which I once used to sail a thousand miles and more further downstream. Like its brother the Salween, this limpid little mountain stream bore no resemblance to the huge muddy river of Laos and Cambodia.

* This prophecy doesn't seem to have been fulfilled.

I searched high and low for petrol, in vain. Rather than risk running out in the middle of the night, I stopped at dusk in a village surrounded by walls, like all the townships in Yunnan, which had much the same aspect as a French town in the Middle Ages must have had. I struck up a conversation in broken English with a local merchant. I told him my trouble. Thanks to a liberal use of gestures, he understood perfectly. I in my turn gathered that he could provide me with petrol, but at an exorbitant price. With my last remaining dollars I might be able to fill up again, which still wouldn't get me further than about fifty miles short of Kunming. I agreed all the same (I had no choice) and took out my wallet. Whatever possessed me to do that?

I had committed the unforgivable crime of *appearing to be in a hurry*. That was enough for the shark to assume a blank expression and start fiddling about with some empty tins in the back of his shop, nodding his head with a sorrowful smile. I had seen his eyes glint when I mentioned petrol. There was a guaranteed profit for him in the deal. But profit was one thing, *courtesy* was another. The rules of Chinese courtesy, established and firmly fixed over the centuries, forbade him to strike a bargain in such an informal manner. He was shocked at my vulgarity and made no effort to conceal it. I should have embarked on a harmless conversation with him and, after an hour of commonplace chat, indirectly switched the subject to the dearth of the fuel that makes motor cars function. Having thus abided by the rules, I could have ventured to insinuate that if someone had the extreme amiability to be good enough to let me have a little petrol, I should be eternally grateful to him. He would then have hinted that perhaps, just to oblige him, one of his friends would consent to produce a few drops of the precious liquid. The ceremony would then have been prolonged by a ritual exchange of compliments. Finally I should have been entitled to slip him the agreed sum, diffidently and with downcast eyes, a sum which he would have refused a good half-dozen times before tucking it away in the pocket of his greatcoat. Then, and only then, should I have obtained satisfaction.

But I was a mere savage who didn't know the first thing about courtesy* and I had stupidly inquired if it was possible to buy some petrol. This delayed me for another night, which I spent once more in the car, after realising that this son of heaven would rather let himself be cut up into small pieces than part forthwith with the few gallons I needed.

Next morning (not too early), after champing at the bit in silence and manifesting due humility, I finally obtained the petrol and drove off towards Kunming, praying to Confucius to enable me to cover the last two hundred miles with an amount of fuel sufficient for a hundred and fifty. I resorted to the Chinese drivers' methods and switched off the engine at the top of every slope.

The wildest and most picturesque stretch of the Burma Road was now coming to an end. The last spot worthy of notice was the little town of Talifu, at the top of a lofty pass, with its sparkling lake dwarfed by snow-covered peaks. I hadn't seen snow for years, and the sight of these mountains, so similar to those in France, brought tears to my eyes.

Talifu was once the capital of the great Moslem district of Yunnan and a large number of Mohammed's disciples were exterminated here by the followers of Confucius. It was also the spot where a market was held that was famous throughout China and to which people came apparently from as far afield as Tibet. But I didn't have the luck to attend this festival.

By this time I had reached the end of the real Road, the Road which the Chinese carved in less than two years, I believe, through these reputedly impenetrable, inhospitable mountains where malaria and cholera reigned supreme. For this task they are said to have assembled more than a million coolies. Many of them died on the spot—fifty thousand, accor-

* Rather like those innocent souls who come to China with the idea of asking questions, fondly imagining that the Chinese reply to the questions they are asked.

ding to one estimate; over a hundred thousand, according to another. I don't think we shall ever know for sure.

I was now driving across the Yunnan Plateau, which was covered in the sort of green grass on which you might expect to find sheep grazing; but I saw only a few herds of cattle. On the other hand,there were quite a lot of crops. Yunnan was rich in vegetables, cereals and fruit. I noticed some peasants tilling some fertile-looking fields. I felt I had come a long way from the stamping ground of the adventurers and pirates. I saw some isolated little farmhouses with thatched roofs, and poultry pecking round them. The landscape reminded me of France and the peasants looked honest and hard-working. Piracy reigned only in the towns and the big commercial centres.

I passed some columns which were not mere ammunition convoys. They were Chinese troops, whose aid the British Government had finally accepted, after much hesitation, and who were making their way towards Mandalay and Burma where, however, they were to arrive too late.

As I feared, and in spite of miraculous feats of economy, I ran out of petrol in the evening some thirty miles short of Kunming. I spent yet another night in the Buick, wondering if I might not have to complete this final lap on foot. I hadn't a cent left and I was dying of hunger.

In the morning, however, I eventually managed to get three gallons of petrol from the driver of an army truck in exchange for my brand-new wrist watch—by no means a bad bargain for him.

It was towards noon, after five days' driving, that I arrived at Kunming, coated from head to toe in brown dust, starving, and using up my last drops of fuel. I had the extraordinary good fortune to run into Long on the main street as soon as I entered the town. He had been here for several days and was wondering what on earth had become of me.

China and the Chinese

I

KUNMING

Kunming (or Yunnanfu), the capital of the province of Yunnan, had a population of fifty thousand before the war. There were now, I believe, two or three hundred thousand inhabitants crammed into the town. To this town, too, the Burma Road had attracted a fair number of racketeers, not to mention the countless Chinese refugees from Malaya, Burma, Shanghai, Hong Kong and Indo-China who had likewise congregated here.

At first I was startled by the cost of living. A suitcase stuffed with dollars was needed instead of a wallet, even for the smallest purchases. I moved in with Long to the Hotel Europe, the only reasonable comfortable one, and where European food was available. A canal ran beneath my room. Tame cormorants used to dive into the murky water and catch small fish for the benefit of an old man who kept watch over them through half-closed eyes.

The hotel was run by a Greek family, all of whom spoke French. The British citizens that we officially were had to be extremely careful and we spoke nothing but English even among ourselves. This was all very well for Long, but I felt my own accent was hard to countenance, even for a Mauritian.

At one time French influence had been fairly pronounced in Yunnan. Even today the Vichy consul, who was still on duty, indulged in a great deal of official activity, while we allies were obliged to lie low. He dazzled the Chinese, apparently, by his style of living and controlled a whole network of Annamite agents.

71

The rest of the French community in Kunming consisted of the staff of the Yunnan Railway Company, whose traffic had been reduced to almost nil since the break with Indo-China, the staff of the French Hospital, and, finally, Monsieur Reclus, who taught our native language at the French School of Yunnan. Our only contact was Reclus, whose loyalty and security were proven. Thanks to him and his knowledge of the country and to his wife, who was Chinese, we avoided many blunders with the local authorities.

Before my departure for China some English friends had told me: 'Don't leave your car unattended for a minute during your journey. Remove and lock up the sweepers of the windscreen wipers, the valve covers and radiator cap when you park. Sleep in the car with one eye open and a revolver by your side.' I had followed this valuable advice all the way to Kunming, and everything had gone well. On my arrival I left the car outside the hotel, in full view of the restaurant, for three minutes, after removing the above-mentioned accessories. Alas, my friends had omitted to add: the hub caps, the arms of the windscreen wipers and the cap of the petrol tank. All these had disappeared on my return. I was forced to go to the junk market on the public square, where I paid a few hundred dollars for some similar spare parts which may indeed have been the very ones that had been stolen. Out of what was displayed there (the provenance of which was an open secret) several complete vehicles could have been assembled.

Long had succeeded in making an impression on the Yunnan notables and Chinese generals. All of them regarded us with a mixture of curiosity and distrust, but they declared themselves ready to help us. The foundations of Free France were now laid in China. Major T., head of the military mission, was to operate in Chungking, assisted by d'Iribarne, who was to join us presently, and Léonard, who had just left Singapore with a case of documents and was at the moment somewhere at sea between Malaya, Sumatra and Indo-China, but whom we expected to turn up shortly. Finally, Professor

May was to be stationed in Kunming. Where he was exactly, no one knew, but he had last been heard of in Rangoon.

Long and I were to leave for the Tonkin frontier, try to re-establish contact with friendly elements in the interior, and later enter Indo-China ourselves if circumstances permitted. The Chinese had promised to provide wireless transmitters and operators, plus an interpreter and a guide. This clandestine activity was beginning to fascinate them and they too now assumed a conspiratorial manner and would only meet us after dark at secret rendezvous. We were to set off as soon as our team had been made up, which would be in a month's time.

While waiting for the men and equipment that were promised to arrive from Chungking, we tried to acquaint ourselves with the country and its inhabitants. Yunnan was, in theory, dependent on the central government of Chiang Kai-shek. The latter's representatives did indeed exercise a certain amount of authority, but not exclusively. The governor of the province was reported to be no more than a superficial supporter of the then master of China and his loyalty was suspect. Under him, power was exercised by a caste of high mandarins who acted as petty economic and financial dictators, feudal lords who were extremely jealous of their privileges.

A little lower down the administrative ladder there was a whole gamut of generals. Never shall I forget the Chinese generals of this region and this period! It was with them we had the most frequent contact and through them we were invited to endless meals, in the course of which all the ritual, all the finer points, all the mysteries of Chinese courtesy were relentlessly revealed.

First of all a good hour would be devoted to an exchange of compliments through the medium of an interpreter, Colonel Cha, a rather picturesque character to whom I shall have further occasion to refer. The host would start off with the usual laudatory remarks about our country. Thereupon Long, who was admirable at this little game, would sing the praises of the New China and General Chiang. The senior general would then reply by extolling Free France and her leader. At this juncture I would feel obliged to interject a word and would elaborate on Long's compliments, which would result in a fresh laudatory offensive on the part of a lesser lordling. There was no reason why it should ever come to an end, and in fact it never did come to an end.

This assault was followed up by a contest in humility and an epic tussle to see who would be the last to go through into the dining room and, after that, the last to take his place at table. The meal would then begin, each course being punctuated by further courtesies. Our hosts did us proud, there was no doubt about it. There would be a score or more of dishes and the cooking was good. In addition to the customary shark's fins and bird's nests, we were introduced to all sorts of unknown victuals and sauces. What never changed was the order of the meal: first, a succession of grilled meat, roast fowl carved into small pieces, Yunnan ham, fish, and a variety of vegetables. The first time, we thought that the meal had finished after this debauch. Not at all; they were merely titbits intended to whet our appetites. It was after this series that the real meal began, consisting invariably of a dish of rice and a boiled chicken served whole in a tureen of broth, from which everyone detached what he could with his chopsticks.

Yet another point of ritual: before the rice, between each course, tradition recommended (and even demanded) that each guest should toss off a small glass of rice spirit ('Chinese wine', as our interpreter called it), but from the moment the rice was on the table, courtesy forbade the drinking of this 'wine'. To do so would have been an abominable social solecism. If anyone wants to know why it is bad form to drink spirits while eating rice, let him go and consult the writings of Confucius.

Colonel Cha, our first interpreter (we had another later), was a remarkable character, as I have already said. A colonel, because this was the lowest rank that could decently be given to an interpreter in China, Cha had spent several years in

France and was immensely proud of it. It was no laughing matter. He appeared to have combined in himself all that was most unwholesome in both civilisations. His knowledge of French was limited to a few coarse phrases picked up, as far as I could gather, in the brothels of Marseilles.

He was attached to the staff of General Li, who himself belonged to the central government in Chungking. Li was quite a different kettle of fish and we deeply regretted not being able to talk to him directly; unfortunately he understood neither French nor English. The indispensable Cha never left us alone for a second. He escorted us whenever we went out to a restaurant. He offered his services to get us (at a high price) anything we needed and protected us from the 'lousy Vichy spies' who, he said, were out to 'bugger us up'.

He was as boastful as a Marseillais, as garrulous as a Gascon and as venal as a Chinese pirate. It was obvious that he took a commission from all the merchants to whom he introduced us. We were inclined to take exception to this at first, then became more tolerant on reflecting that his pay as a colonel in this strange country was a hundred and seventy-six dollars a month, which did not enable him to buy even a decent meal. He had to live on his wits, as indeed did most of the generals themselves.

Obliged at every turn to rely on him as an intermediary, we made little headway. Chungking kept promising to send us our transmitters, but nothing arrived. We spent our time going from one Chinese banquet to another, which soon began to pall.

The strength of the Free French Mission in China was presently increased by the arrival of some new members (up to now there had been just three of us). Professor May, a surgeon in civilian life, tired of broadcasting periodical imprecations from Rangoon for the benefit of Vichy listeners, turned up in Kunming at the wheel of a jeep. In the same convoy, and each with a similar vehicle, came Léonard, who had finally reached dry land after a perilous voyage across the Indian

75

Ocean, and d'Iribarne, who had likewise driven a jeep all the way in spite of having only one arm. Since the Japanese invasion of Burma the Americans had started distributing jeeps to everyone as though they were chocolates, at the rate of one per person.

Léonard gave us the latest news from Saigon. He had left a few days before the capitulation. Others had escaped when the Japanese were already in the town, on Chinese junks, sampans, even canoes, and had succeeded (some of them) in reaching India, after an eventful voyage, in spite of the enemy aircraft.

D'Iribarne and Léonard moved on immediately to Chungking, where Major T. had summoned them. May stayed behind with us in Kunming, where still more Chinese banquets were given in his honour.

Apart from the Chinese generals, we saw hardly anyone except a few Englishmen belonging to a clandestine organisation and who were in the know about our own activities. Among these was a man named Birnie, who in civilian life had been the director of a plantation company in Indo-China (yet another planter!). He had handed in his resignation on the arrival of the Japanese, joined up in Malaya and had been working in close liaison with us ever since. He had brought his wife with him to Kunming, where they had arrived at the same time as Long, but they both found it difficult to adapt themselves to Chinese customs and it was not long before they left.

There was also L., the assistant to the British consul. He had spent ten years of his life in China, spoke Chinese better than any son of heaven, and spent his time fulminating against the Europeans who, having sped through this country in a few days, could hardly wait on their return to write a book about China. He was a very pleasant fellow.

In our anxiety to abide by our cover-up story, we were familiar with no Frenchman apart from Reclus. Occasionally, however, we did meet another, a man named S., who ran the only decent garage and whom we had to see about a repair job. The scene deserves to be described: playing our parts as British citizens, we started off by asking for an interpreter. He was an Annamite, who spoke very bad English and poor French. Long explained what we wanted in Shakespeare's language and we listened, exasperated but forcing ourselves to remain impassive, to his French translation which was completely inaccurate. The trouble was that S. was a good fellow and would insist on convincing us of his pro-British feelings. The conversation, through the interpreter's howlers, became more and more involved. We tried out a few words in French, which Long pronounced in an incredible English accent, making them utterly incomprehensible. S. burst out with a sentence in English which he had learned by heart. The interpreter gave up in despair and broke into Annamite. This scene was enacted every time we brought our car to the garage. I don't think old S. ever suspected our real nationality. Thanks to the interpreter, I believe he finally took us for Russians.

After the excitement of the journey and the initial thrill of being in China, I began to find the waiting monotonous and to doubt if we would ever secure our ends in this country in which the main virtue appeared to be patience. For two pins I would have gladly followed Birnie's example. One fine morning, in a fit of disgust, he abandoned China to the Chinese, Indo-China to whoever wanted to have her, and decided to make his way home, the only place where any useful work was done. His departure even occasioned a farcical little scene. One hour before take-off, his wife discovered that the aircraft on which they had booked was piloted by a Chinese. Nothing could be done to persuade her to board this plane and I think her husband secretly agreed with her. This was no reflection on Mrs Birnie's courage, still less on her husband's—he had undertaken several extremely hazardous missions in the 1914–1918 war—it was simply that they both felt *uncomfortable* at the idea of travelling in a plane with a Chinese pilot. I might have felt equally disturbed if I had been in their place . . . We were frightful colonialists.

77

Thus I began to wonder if it wouldn't be better if we all went to England ourselves, but Long had more moral fibre. He had set his heart on Indo-China and refused to be discouraged. As though to justify his attitude, we were suddenly informed that our wireless operators had been dispatched from Chungking, together with their equipment.

We couldn't have chosen a worse moment for the operation we had in mind. The Japanese were masters of the Dutch East Indies, the Philippines and part of New Guinea, and we were even beginning to feel anxious about Australia. On the mainland, after seizing Rangoon, they had marched north without meeting any resistance and were now approaching Mandalay. Professor May, who was often pessimistic, predicted their imminent entry into Yunnan. Indo-China was almost completely surrounded.

April, 1942

Our departure for the frontier was finally arranged. General Li produced a new interpreter named Fan, who was to accompany us, for there was no question of taking Colonel Cha along—thank heaven! Fan began by apologising for speaking French very badly. And after a few days we were to discover that he spoke Chinese badly as well, at least the Chinese of Yunnan. But he seemed a nice chap.

Our team consisted of Long, promoted to senior general; myself, junior general; interpreter Fan, who was to put on the badges of rank of a colonel as soon as we had left Kunming (while waiting to sport those of a general in circumstances to which I shall refer later); Mr Ho and Mr Ha, our wireless operators, the latter fortunately speaking a few words of English; and finally a guide, a Chinese from Yunnan, who knew the frontier region and had useful contacts there.

Our equipment consisted of two portable transmitters with enough batteries to last several months; a crate of tinned food marked 'Made in England' which Birnie, with typical English foresight, had trundled all the way from Singapore and handed over to us; camp beds, blankets and mosquito nets; quinine and a few medical supplies; and, last 'but by no means least, a huge packing case which, judging by appearances, must contain a Provencal wardrobe or Breton cabinet but which, in fact, enclosed only another wireless set intended for our friends in Indo-China—a touching but painfully cumbersome gift from the clandestine organisation in Singapore, which Long had succeeded, heaven knows how, in transporting all the way here. All this filled a whole truck which General Li had put at our disposal together with a driver.

The preparations for our departure were conducted in a renewed outbreak of mystery. Colonel Cha wore darker and darker uniforms whenever he came to see us. Once again we had to use him as an intermediary to change some money, purchase a few utensils and have some packs made which could be carried on mule-back. Once again we paid through the nose.

Everything was ready at last. Mr Long and Mr Rule had become technical advisers to the Chinese Government. Advisers on what? I never discovered. Our English names, which did not look sufficiently complicated, had been translated into Chinese and we were now equipped with documents which would ensure us safe passage and assistance throughout the province of Yunnan. Each general suggested some fresh stratagem to shroud us more and more in mystery. There was talk of disguising us as missionaries, of making us don false beards, of clothing us in Chinese uniforms. Finally we merely assumed our titles of technical advisers.

Our last Chinese meal in Kunming. We sincerely thanked General Li, who had clearly done his utmost to help us. He represented, I believe, a class of the Young China that was worthy of interest and respect, utterly different from Cha's and even more so from that of the high mandarins who lorded it over the province and bled it white. This at least was the impression he made on me.

2

MONGTSEU

With our staff and baggage piled into the back of the truck, we climbed in beside the driver and headed south. In a jeep which he had just been allotted and which he drove most erratically, Colonel Cha escorted us for several miles, as was only right and proper for guests of our distinction. In this case security had to yield to courtesy. Then he turned round, waved his arms in farewell and we left him far behind in the dust. This was the moment Fan chose to produce his colonel's badges of rank.

We skirted the lakes bordering Kunming, the realm of wild duck, and drove until nightfall in the direction of Mongtseu. This was the last outpost of civilisation before the frontier. From there we would have to continue on mule-back.

We stopped at the outskirts of a village teeming with military and Fan set off in search of accommodation for us. He had the fantastic idea of making us sleep in a sort of window-less stable, but we strongly objected and set up our camp beds on the side of the road. Fan was dismayed at our shameless-ness: the rules of etiquette did not permit two great generals like ourselves to sleep out in the open. He consoled himself, however, with a meal generously washed down with a spirit distilled from a sweet pinkish fruit and which he called 'Yun-nan wine'. We spent a fairly peaceful night, disturbed only once by some prowling figures. Long, who had wakened with a start, cocked his revolver, and this sound, which was no doubt familiar to them, was enough to put the nosy-parkers to flight.

We set off again in the morning through a region no less

chaotic than Upper Burma. Mountains, nothing but mountains, and beyond still more mountains, but all extremely varied. We were now driving across a plateau dotted with huge blocks of granite which looked rather like the Baie d'Along minus the sea; this was succeeded by a smiling valley, then some passes and further valleys, followed by further plateaux; finally some hillocks of oddly carved, contorted rocks which called to mind certain corners of the Provençal Alpilles.

The road, which was fairly good to start with, had petered out into a sandy track with deep pot-holes. We started passing convoys of mules, the commonest form of transport in southern Yunnan. The animals were not accustomed to motorised vehicles and our truck caused havoc among the caravans while the muleteers shouted and cursed us.

We were hoping to reach the end of this lap by nightfall but, just as our interpreter spoke very bad French, so our driver handled the truck deplorably. Our anxiety, however, was soon dispelled. Everything turns out all right in China: the driver had spent some time in Singapore and spoke a little Malay, so he acted henceforth as our interpreter and I took over the wheel.

As for Fan, he seemed delighted. He gave us to understand that through living with us he would at last be able to learn French. Apparently this was the only reason he had accepted his assignment.

We reached Mongtseu in pitch dark, after losing our way several times. There once had been a comfortable hotel here, but it had been closed since the war. All we could find was a sort of inn in which men and mules dossed down cheek by jowl. Once again we chose to camp outside the town, after draining a half bottle of whisky which L. had given us before we left. We drank a loving cup with Fan, for we had given him rather a hard time during his unfortunate attempts to inquire about the right road. He seemed blissfully happy and declared in a triumphant tone that 'he did not wish for our arms'. After puzzling over this remark for a moment—for there had been no question of our giving him our weapons—we deciphered his message: he did not wish us harm; in other words, he was full of the best intentions towards us. So much the better.

We spent our second night in the open uneventfully, waked only at first light by a buffalo sniffing round our camp beds. We sent our colonel interpreter off to reconnoiter the town and establish contact with the generals of the local army who were to help us on our way. Contact was quickly established. The authorities had been informed of our arrival by General An, the supreme military chief of Yunnan, whom we had met in Kunming and whose powers extended throughout the region that we were about to cross.

On his recommendation we got in touch with the Customs service, which was apparently a most redoubtable type of semi-civilian, semi-military organisation. At one time almost all the commercial traffic between Indo-China and Yunnan had to pass through the Mongtseu Customs. There was no longer any official commerce, but I assume the clandestine traffic was sufficient to justify the maintenance of a substantial administration: French cigarettes fetched a high price throughout the province and the piastre had a favourable rate of exchange. Some of the generals in Kunming had offered us 'French wine', which turned out to be 3-star Martell, whose provenance was an open secret.

We were introduced to General Hong, who welcomed us like grand mandarins. He put a building at our disposal for as long as we were to remain in Mongtseu and undertook to find us mules and porters. He was full of apologies because his superior, General Sun, was away at the moment, but we were cordially invited to spend the evening and *have a bath* in the general's house, where his wife would be very honoured to receive us. Although somewhat surprised, we hastened to accept.

The rest of the day was spent unloading our truck and making a few purchases while Fan saw about the convoy of mules. Among other things, we bought some heavy quilted bedding, for the nights were icy cold in the region which we were about to confront. Fan acquitted himself well. The caravan would be ready in two days' time and, apart from the mounts, would include two foot porters, selected from the hardiest in the town, to carry the famous Singapore transmitter whose size precluded its being transported on a pack-saddle.

The ground floor of the building in which General Hong had quartered us was occupied by soldiers. Unfortunately there was not a single water tap on our floor. Having discovered the only pump in the yard, we dowsed ourselves under it before the eyes of the astonished soldiery. This was a minor scandal: Fan was most upset. That two generals should have a shower in public violated all the rites, all the laws of courtesy. According to the rules, they should be brought a tub of boiling water and towels the size of a handkerchief, in a hermetically sealed room, so that they might sponge their brows in dignity. Our behaviour really made him despair; he himself lost face in the eyes of the soldiers. For the rest of the journey he was to spend half the time running after us to avoid similar blunders.

We spent a memorable evening at General Sun's. Fan, who was keeping in touch with the authorities, came and fetched us at eleven o'clock at night, puffed out with a sense of his own importance, just as we were beginning to think there had been a change in the programme. But no: the general's wife insisted that we should go over and have a bath.

We entered a vast room furnished in half-Chinese, half-European style. The chairs were lined up against the wall as though on parade. Mrs Sun seemed fearfully bashful. She was a ravishing young Chinese woman, wearing a green European dress. Blushing and stammering, she paid us a compliment, which Fan translated as best he could, and asked us to be seated. Our colonel gave us to understand that the bath was being made ready. And indeed we could hear a clatter of buckets on the first floor and, through the half-open door, I caught sight of a column of servants forming a chain as though they were extinguishing a fire.

The time passed, slowly. After the usual exchange of compliments we sat in a daze, almost dozing in our chairs. We should have liked to put the general's wife at her ease, but it was not so easy in these surroundings and with these onlookers, for the room had gradually filled up with solemn mandarins with goatees, their hands snugly tucked into the sleeves of their padded robes. I would never have believed there were Chinese so typically Chinese. I almost expected to see a figure in pigtails appear.

They drifted in as silently as wraiths, bowed towards us and towards the lady of the house, went and sat down on the chairs against the wall which were apparently reserved for them, and sat staring at us without saying a word. These were the town dignitaries, probably the high aristocracy of Mongtseu, who had been invited in our honour. We must have intrigued them immensely, maybe shocked them, with our travelling clothes but, like well brought-up people, they did not show it. I must confess I was impressed and intimidated by their behaviour and their dignity, as I was by General Hong's welcome, by the efficiency which reigned in his office and by the signs of respect vouchsafed by his soldiers.

The first bath was now ready, for this was what all the fuss was about. Preceded by a very pompous servant, Long went up to the first floor while I remained a solitary target for these statues frozen along the wall. It was an hallucinating experience and I was pleased when he presently came down again. I had to wait a good hour longer for the second bath to be prepared. Eventually my turn came and I was ushered up to the first floor. There, I was in for a shock: I found myself in an absolutely modern, not to say luxurious, bathroom equipped with every amenity—except running water. There was not even the most elementary plumbing. This accounted for all the bustle: no doubt every servant in the house had been requisitioned to fill the bath to the brim with hot water. Hot, did

I say? It was boiling! I dipped the tip of my little finger in it and scalded myself atrociously. An egg would have cooked in it in three minutes and, since there was no cold water to cool it, I resigned myself to giving up this bath, which I was longing for and which in this place probably represented the utmost of what could be done to oblige a guest of distinction. No doubt, too, Fan had spread it about that we liked washing.

Be that as it may, I did not want to offend the general's wife or make her lose face. I resorted to subterfuge. I melted down enough soap to make the water cloudy (holding it with the tips of my fingers). I took off my clothes, rumpled the towels and after a decent interval of time sorrowfully dressed again, reflecting deeply on the subject of Chinese courtesy.

This sort of incident was to be repeated, with a few variations, throughout our journey. Every tub, accompanied by the traditional handkerchief-towels brought to us by zealous servants, was to contain a liquid verging on boiling point. The water we were given to drink in the poorer villages where there was no tea was likewise boiling. Only peasants, Fan explained, used cold water. Hot water was an outward sign of wealth and power. I suppose tepid water was reserved for the middle classes; in any case, great generals like ourselves could be offered only water at a temperature of a hundred degrees centigrade. This is what courtesy demanded; we could do no more than submit.

We left Sun's house about two in the morning, thanking the blushing general's wife effusively. After all, it was the intention that mattered and many a French custom would seem ridiculous to the people of Yunnan.

We slept only a short time, for we had been invited to breakfast at seven next morning by General Hong. Seven in the morning for an official banquet! Mongtseu was certainly full of surprises. But eating at any time of the day was a widespread habit in this region. Later on, whenever our caravan arrived in some out-of-the-way hamlet in the middle of the night, exhausted and asleep on our feet, we would still have to partake of a traditional Chinese dinner with the authorities before being entitled to retire.

This meal, to which General Hong and the senior Customs officers invited us, remains forever stamped on my memory. It was one of the best and strangest I have ever eaten. It consisted of nothing but broth. Yes, nothing but broth and it didn't pall in the least. There were at least twenty different kinds of consommé, each with a different flavour: chicken soup, duck soup, pork soup, beef soup, bullock soup, buffalo soup, fish soup, each likewise containing a different variety of vermicelli. It was a real feast and we did justice to it in spite of the early hour, as well as to the little glasses of rice spirit to which I was beginning to grow accustomed.

Our departure had been fixed for the day after next. Until then there was nothing for us to do in Mongtseu but wander among the seething crowd of Chinese and mules: wretched overloaded Yunnan mules, equipped with what was once a pack but was now a cat's cradle of wooden boards, string and wire, filthy dirty, never groomed, toiling day and night up and down goat paths, and turning an envious eye on the sleek little ponies replete with hay and oats belonging to the generals and Customs officials.

Mongtseu was apparently the rallying point of the caravans that came from the south laden with mysterious bundles. I believe it was one of the biggest smuggling centres: contraband cigarettes and opium were important sources of income for the high mandarins and senior generals who controlled all the clandestine organisations that came under the heading of the Customs Service.

Another impression was the facility and simplicity with which the authorities solved the most complicated problems. Here, for example, is a story which General Hong told us, not without a hint of pride. There used to be a big aerodrome and aeronautical college in Mongtseu. The Japanese having come and bombed these installations somewhat too often for the liking of the masters of the town, the latter merely did away with the college and converted the aerodrome to pasture land. Long was full of admiration for this typical Chinese rejoinder.

On the eve of our departure there was a final banquet at General An's (Great An, as our interpreter called him, to distinguish him from his brother, Little An) who had just arrived from Kunming. He was a person of considerable consequence, the most powerful man in the region, I believe, and he had the best cook in the whole of Yunnan. The dinner was delicious. Mr Ho and Mr Ha, who were part of our entourage, were invited by virtue of this to the table of the High and Mighty, and so was Fan. The general had his own personal interpreter, who translated his master's compliments in very decent English. Fan, relegated to a secondary role, concentrated on the food. Numerous toasts were drunk to the success of our enterprise. After dinner General An introduced his son, of whom he was very proud because he was beginning to learn English. He seemed a very bright lad. It was rather like a family gathering in a well-to-do household in France.

We left Mongtseu next day, on a bright sunny morning, threading our way through the blossoming fruit trees which grew in profusion round the town.

3

CHINESE TRACKS

Our caravan consisted of six mules for the baggage; a so-called saddle horse for each member of the team; two porters on foot for the monumental transmitter, that indestructible and cumbersome present from the Singapore clandestine organisation; and finally an escort, graciously provided by General An, of half a dozen soldiers armed to the teeth and an officer who was not entitled to a mount (he was a very junior lieutenant) but who ingeniously clung to the mules' tails when going up hill.

The two porters deserve special mention. They were Hounis, worthy representatives of one of those countless tribes ('savage tribes', Fan called them) of maybe Tibetan origin, which pullulate all over southern Yunnan and northern Indo-China, the most important by far being the Thais, whom we were to encounter shortly. The Hounis are far less numerous, less well known, and yet how picturesque! They inhabit the summits of the mountains, in huts on stilts, away from the other natives. They do a little hunting and fishing with primitive implements, but above all they are expert smugglers and are used for this purpose by the local tycoons. Dressed in black, with a turban of the same colour wound round their heads, invisible in the dark, they worm their way through the impenetrable under-growth, carrying loads which would crush a European. For all this, with their placid nature, they are treated rather like slaves by all the other natives and in particular by the Chinese.

Over and over again I was to admire the resistance of the Chinese soldiers in our escort who without batting an eyelid would march twenty or twenty-five miles at a stretch over the mountains, with nothing to eat but a handful of rice; but I am at a loss for words to express my feelings towards the feats performed by our two Hounis during this five days' journey. They would start off at the same time as the caravan, carrying on a litter the famous transmitter which was so heavy that Long and I could scarcely lift it a few inches from the ground. Trotting briskly along, they would soon outpace the horses, mules and escort. We did not see them again for the rest of the day. In the evening, when we ourselves arrived dog-tired at the halting place, we would find them squatting beside the crate with which they had been entrusted, solemnly smoking their water pipes which, with opium, was their only vice. They had arrived long before us, eaten a handful of rice and started smoking while waiting for us to appear. They would remain squatting on their heels like this, often for most of the night. It was their method of resting after their daily labours. In the morning they would set off again, fresh and alert, on a further lap. Not once did they complain about the weight of their load. They did all this for a pittance, and when one day I offered them a packet of Chinese tobacco they thanked me effusively in a language that no one could understand.

Thus we left Mongtseu. Fan began showing off at once and galloped ahead. The Yunnan guide sat astride his horse with an ease that I envied. Mr Ho and Mr Ha, who were towns-folk, were not at all used to such exercise, but their position as technicians almost obliged them to prove that they could turn their hands to anything and they did not acquit them-selves too badly.

As for me, I was far from happy. I had done a little riding before, even over rough ground, but one couldn't reasonably apply the term 'rough ground' to this series of razor-sharp rocks and sheer drops followed by ascents through prickly brushwood where the path was invisible, to these torrents which, if one was lucky, one crossed on the back of one's mount but more often than not clinging on to its tail. Nor could one apply the word 'horse' to this strange sort of animal with jutting ribs which climbed like a goat, scampered like a squirrel or slithered like a snake, following the demands of the terrain; any more than one could compare a proper saddle to this tangle of leather, cord and wire which kept sticking into my backside. Long, albeit a fine horseman, seemed scarcely more comfortable than I.

The soldiers of the escort marched along at a brisk pace. At the start, on the flat, they were obliged to move at the double to keep up with the horses. They were now being compensated and frequently had to stop for us to catch up with them. We could easily have done without this escort, but General An had forced it on us. He no doubt felt responsible for our security and, if anything happened to us, it would probably mean dishonour for him. Moreover, the region was anything but secure. As we crossed the first ridge above Mongtseu, I noticed some posts of militia hired by the local land-owners to guard the maize fields.

Then again, we had to have an escort because we were in China and because it was not proper for the High and Mighty to wander about the countryside without a few men-at-arms to mark their distinction.

Our objective was a military post called Pin-Ku-Yin, high up in the mountains and still some distance from the frontier. The Chinese had chosen it for us, promising that from there we would be able to infiltrate some agents into Indo-China.

After a fairly short stage we reached the first stopping-place in the afternoon: it was quite a small post commanded by a colonel who, informed by radio of our approach, had spruced up to receive us. We just had time to cast a compassionate glance at our two Hounis squatting by their crate before being ushered into a bamboo hut where we found the inevitable basin of boiling water, the usual handkerchief-towels and the traditional meal waiting for us.

There now began an undeclared and epic tussle between the European element and the Chinese element as represented by the officer who received us and especially by our friend Fan. We had noticed a stretch of clear water close by and we resorted to every trick under the sun to escape for five minutes and have a swim. In vain; it was Fan who won this round, but we were to redeem ourselves at the next halt. He divined our perfidious plan; he did not leave us for a second and literally pushed us towards the table. The incident of the shower we had had in public in Mongtseu had made him too miserable. Once more we sat down to yet another Chinese banquet, similar to the previous ones, at which the colonel did the honours.

After the meal, which went on rather late, we were invited to sleep in a stuffy little room with tiny windows. Once again the open air and our camp beds would have suited us better, but our interpreter assumed such a suppliant air that we yielded and spent the night in this hovel.

The second lap was much the same as the first, only worse; the track became still rougher and climbed continuously. We were not to stop climbing until we reached Pin-Ku-Yin. But we hadn't got there yet; the next halt was the village of Minhao on the banks of the Red River. I covered a large part of the way on foot and even on all fours, leaving my horse to fend for itself.

Mountains, still more mountains! Sometimes, when the undergrowth was less thick, we caught a glimpse of the two Hounis climbing briskly high above our heads. It had rained during the night and the horses stumbled and slipped at every step. They always succeeded in recovering their foothold, however, just as one was beginning to imagine them at the bottom of the precipice.

We arrived dead-beat at Minhao shortly before sunset. Here, disregarding Fan's entreaties this time, we plunged into the Red River which at this point hardly deserved the name since the water was crystal clear. Our interpreter was the only person to be scandalised. The natives of the village seemed delighted and the soldiers of the escort, after a short hesitation, followed our example. The two townsmen, Mr Ho and Mr Ha, pursed their lips superciliously. In a final attempt to put an end to this scandal straight away, Fan told us a grim story about giant tortoises which, he said, haunted the river and dragged bathers to the bottom; but this had no effect on us. The two Hounis, silent and inscrutable as ever, sat smoking their pipes at the water's edge, vaguely bewildered by our outrageous behaviour. Their job was to carry a crate across the mountains and not to play the fool in icy water.

I believe it was at Minhao that I first conceived the idea of an original method of infiltrating secretly into Indo-China. It occurred to me that if I floated down-stream I would arrive at Lao-Kay, the frontier town, and from there the current would take me on quite naturally to Hanoi. But I shelved this idea for the time being. The Red River was bound to be closely guarded on the confines of the frontier.

I can't remember much about Minhao apart from one or two isolated constructions I noticed on the famous Yunnan Railway running from Hanoi to Kunming. The Chinese had removed the rails since the arrival of the Japanese in Indo-China.

Apart from the swim, this halt was much the same as the previous one—Chinese meal, basin of boiling water before and after the meal, sleep in a hut which had been carefully sealed so as to admit no air from outside. The next three halts were identical. We continued to climb, higher and higher. When, on the evening of the fifth day, after a final scramble up some larger rocks which formed a sort of staircase, we eventually arrived at Pin-Ku-Yin, we had the impression of having reached the topmost pinnacles of China.

4

PIN-KU-YIN

Pin-Ku-Yin! A merciless spot, a crag perpetually shrouded in mephitic mists, a mountain forsaken by man and God alike! Here we mouldered away for several months, together with a handful of Chinese soldiers whose unlucky star had assigned them to this post.

Pin-Ku-Yin is situated at the top of a pass. It is reached (by anyone so witless as to want to reach it) from the Mongtseu side by the track that we had followed, from the Indo-China side by an almost sheer cliff. Here the Chinese military authorities had established a post, a post which was once quite important, judging by the number of hutments, now falling to pieces and mostly unoccupied. Malaria, together with a mysterious disease which makes the neck swell, so Fan said, had decimated the garrison and the casualties had not been replaced. There remained about thirty soldiers who waited with resignation for a similar fate under the command of Colonel Song, the lord and master of the place. Some distance from the camp, overlooking the valley, a cemetery consisting of a surprising number of graves bore witness to the gentleness of the climate.

Pin-Ku-Yin was shrouded in cloud at least two days out of three. One had to scramble up the mountains overlooking the pass, as we did, to catch a glimpse of the sun. An icy damp crept into everyone and everything, and had gradually rotted away the thatch roofs of the hutments. There could have been no better choice for a centre of conspiracy. I have always suspected the Chinese generals of suggesting this place to us on account of its sinister atmosphere.

Nevertheless we were received with the customary cordiality by Colonel Song, whose guests we were to be for over a month. Song was a perfect host. He was silent and withdrawn. He had only one fault: he spat—a fearful habit in a race with such fine manners. The male Chinese of Yunnan spits in his own house, spits in his friends' houses, spits in restaurants, at table, in bed, in the cinema, in battle, in pursuit of game, at rest. The female Chinese spits while doing the housework, spits while darning socks, spits while making love. In the streets of a Chinese village gobs of spittle rain down like primary truths. At the end of every meal there's a regular competition in spitting among all the guests, whereas picking one's teeth without concealing one's face behind a napkin is an outrageous breach of etiquette. Such were the Chinese I knew; such was Colonel Song. There was nothing to be done about it.

We unloaded the baggage and sent the mules and drivers back to Mongtseu. Our Hounis set off on the return journey that very evening at their usual brisk pace. We moved into one of the abandoned huts. Water dripped through the straw roof and we were obliged to fix an awning above our camp beds. But this was nothing; it was not long before the real scourge of Pin-Ku-Yin revealed itself. No sooner had we lain down and put the candle out than we underwent our first assault from the rats.

There was a hellish cavalcade above our heads, as though a legion of demons had taken possession of the hut. Presently, moreover, this horde invaded the beaten earth which served as a floor, then our beds. I heard Long give a startled yell. A rat had bitten the tip of his nose. There was no question of sleeping; we were obliged to clap our hands every five minutes to drive them away. They were barely disturbed by this noise; they grew accustomed to everything. They grew accustomed even to the gleam of the candle which we had to relight. We could only snatch a little sleep by pulling the blankets right over our heads.

Next day, however, we got down to work. The first thing was to re-establish contact with the outside world, for since our departure we had had no news of our friends or of the war. Mr Ho and Mr Ha set up their transmitters in an adjoining hut which they shared with Fan. They succeeded in contacting Chungking and Kunming almost at once. We sent Major T. an account of our trip and what information we had gathered on the way. We asked Professor May, who was at Kunming, for cigarettes and rat poison. We expected to have replies within forty-eight hours; we had to wait eight days. It seemed there was no proper liaison between the Chinese posts, who acknowledged our signals straight away, and the French mission.

For our mail and supplies, we would have to rely on our Yunnanese guide, who would shuttle to and fro between Kunming and Pin-Ku-Yin. He did not appear at all alarmed at the idea of having to spend his time on mule-back and set off after only two days' rest.

We had news of the war that very day from two separate sources: Radio Saigon, to which we listened through earphones (a strange sensation for me to hear this station here!) and a Radio Chungking bulletin which Fan translated for us. On the whole the situation in the Far East sounded anything but encouraging. In Burma the Japanese had reached the mountains, taken Mandalay and Lashio and were now marching up the Road. There was fighting at this moment at Wantung, on the Chinese frontier, where for the first time I had seen the celestial flag hoisted.

I took a keen interest in their progress along this route, which I remembered in detail. One of their thrusts was directed northwards, in the direction of Mitkina, with the intention of cutting the last communications between India and China. The English troops then performed one of the great feats of the war. Without ammunition, without supplies, they marched over reputedly impassable mountains and succeeded in reaching India, where the general commanding them declared he would come back one day by the same route. He was to keep his word in 1945, when he returned to liberate Burma.

Meanwhile the Japanese were at the gates of India and Yunnan—Yunnan, whose loyalty was more and more doubtful, as could be seen from various signs. A journey to Kunming by Chiang Kai-shek seemed to restore the situation for the time being and some fairly substantial forces were sent to the Burma frontier.

The Philippines had been conquered after stout resistance; the Dutch East Indies did not last long. The slogan of Great East Asia had been launched. Passionate appeals were broadcast every day from Singapore, rechristened Shonan, addressed to the Indian brethren, the Chinese brethren, the Malay brethren, the Burmese brethren, urging them to unite under the banner of the Rising Sun. This seemed to be the moment for us to take action.

With the help of Colonel Song and through the medium of numerous minor notables in the region (nothing could be done here without countless intermediaries) we dispatched a Chinese emissary into Indo-China. He was to bring us back information on the frontier region, take a message to a friend in Hanoi and try to get another through to Saigon. There was nothing else we could do but wait for his return with patience.

The days were long in Pin-Ku-Yin: long, damp and cold, as I shall never weary of repeating. When the clouds lifted, the mist came down instead. We lived enveloped in a shroud of dripping water. We applied ourselves as best we could to shaking off the depression that haunted us.

In spite of Fan, who had no doubt been entrusted by the powers that be with our security and was horrified each time we set foot outside our hut, we went for a few excursions. We climbed both of the two peaks overlooking Pin-Ku-Yin. It was tough going, but we were amply compensated for our pains. Once the blanket of mist hanging above the pass lay

below us, we found the blue sky of Yunnan above our heads.
Two parallel valleys, hedged in by cliffs, ran down towards
Indo-China. They met a long way beneath us to form the
Nam-Na, a stream which crosses the frontier and then flows
into the Black River. Nam-Na, Black River, Red River—once
again I found myself thinking that therein lay the natural
route to Hanoi.

This was our daily routine: excursions, rat hunts (we eventually decimated the beasts) and exercises every morning
under the amused eyes of the soldiers in the camp. They too
were kept on the hop by Colonel Song, for whom the replen-
ishment of supplies (a fatigue that entailed a daily fifteen-mile
march over the mountains to the nearest village) was not sufficient exercise. They also paraded for physical training, which
almost always took place in the evening and often went on
until long after dark. It was a strange mixture of gymnastics,
complicated rifle drill and bayonet training, accompanied
invariably by savage yells. Then came the national anthem, to
which we listened in the dark with a certain amount of relief,
for it marked the end of the parade and meant that we might
at last be able to get some sleep. But the Chinese themselves
never slept and we would hear them chatting and laughing,
sometimes until dawn.

We soon grew tired of killing rats and set out in search of
other game, armed with an old rifle that L. had got for us in
Kunming. But even the wild animals had deserted the region
of Pin-Ku-Yin and we always came back empty-handed. We
were therefore extremely surprised one day when Colonel Song
solemnly invited us to a shooting party, on an exceptional
morning when the sun had appeared. He had equipped himself with two army rifles and sent ahead four armed soldiers,
an escort that was just sufficient for a big military chief. I was
curious to know what game he hoped to find. As I expected,
we saw neither bird nor beast. Song knew perfectly well, in
fact, that the mountain was deserted. His shooting party was a
manifestation of art for art's sake.

When he had solemnly dragged us up hill and down dale for a reasonable length of time, he stopped and invited us to a test of marksmanship. The target was a tree trunk overhanging the valley. He showed supreme indifference for a peasant who happened to be tilling his fields directly in the line of fire a few hundred yards further down, and with remarkable composure loosed off round after round. We followed suit, moreover, with equal lack of ceremony. None of us hit the tree trunk. As for the wretched serf below, it was up to him to take cover. I hope he did so at once; no one ever went to make sure.

We had all our meals at Colonel Song's table. The menu was not very varied. It was a far cry from the banquets to which the generals in Kunming had accustomed us; now there was only rice, a boiled chicken, and sometimes a few stringy vegetables. We began to lose weight in spite of drawing more and more frequently on the supplies of tinned food from Burma.

In the evening, to ward off the damp, we used to light a big fire on the beaten earth floor inside our hut. The smoke escaped through whatever aperture it could find. We would invite our Chinese colleagues to join us so as to get better acquainted. Those evenings are indelibly imprinted on my memory. We would roast ourselves voluptuously while brewing up Birnie's tinned coffee. Colonel Song would sit there in silence, muffled up in his greatcoat, never opening his mouth except to spit into the flames. The townsman Mr Ho remained somewhat stiff and formal, whereas Mr Ha, a younger and more natural man, attended to the kettle. All of us would listen attentively to Colonel Fan, who considered that his position as interpreter entitled him to hold forth without drawing breath. He had made some progress in French, as he hoped, and on our side we were becoming familiar with his colourful jargon.

Handing us a cup, he would say, 'Eat some coffee, it's good for wealth,' by which he meant it was good for the health. One day he also said: 'Today's the anniversary of my rebirth.' This time he had to explain what he meant before we could understand. Two years before, to the very day, Fan had been in Chungking, which was then being heavily bombarded. During the raids the population used to take shelter in a sort of natural grotto in the side of the hill, the entrance to which could be sealed off by a narrow door. On that day, during an alert, there were several hundred people in the shelter. Panic broke out for some reason or other and the crowd stampeded, blocking the exit; almost everyone died of asphyxiation. Fan, who would have been there had he not been prevented by some chance incident, called it the day of his rebirth. On another occasion he remarked, in connection with something someone had mentioned: 'That was the year I passed my aerodrome,' by which he meant some mysterious exam, for he had once been a student.

Very often, when he failed to understand what we told him, with our nerves strained by the atmosphere of Pin-Ku-Yin, we felt on the verge of exasperation and made no attempt to conceal it. Then he would come out with a certain phrase, which never varied—a reaction which always succeeded in disarming us. Just as Long was on the point of exploding with irritation, he would assume his most woebegone air and, with an inimitable intonation that oddly called to mind Grock's famous 'sans blague', would gently murmur this sybilline question which had no connection whatever with the subject: 'In which country?' Our annoyance never withstood this phrase or the tone in which it was uttered.*

Sometimes, too, aggravated by the society of the Chinese, we would spend the evening alone together, exchanging gloomy remarks for most of the time, fulminating against Chungking, which did not reply to our signals, against Kunming, which kept sending indecipherable messages and against the slowness of the Chinese and French organisations. We had

* I feel remorse now at the recollection of how we poked fun at him. What ridiculous mistakes we would have made if we had tried to speak Chinese! Admittedly, it would never have occurred to us to volunteer as interpreters.

99

run out of cigarettes and couldn't find a single one in this country, through which, I am certain, crate after crate passed clandestinely every night. This was not calculated to raise our morale.

At last we received a reply from T. and a regular radio link was established; but we didn't have much to communicate. Our Yunnanese came back from Kunming with our mail, but it contained nothing of interest. In the evening we summed up the situation. Pin-Ku-Yin was probably the ideal place in which to lie low and no doubt that was why the Chinese had chosen it for us, but it was more or less impossible to get any proper work done. We were liable to remain buried up here and moulder away until the end of the war. Long decided to make a clean sweep, leave this sinister pass and move our base closer to the frontier. I agreed with enthusiasm.

May, 1942

We detailed Fan to make a reconnaissance, after briefing him thoroughly. He went off with one of Colonel Song's officers who was familiar with the country and put on the badges of rank of a major for the occasion. He was to go as far as Muong-La, a Thai village situated on the banks of the Nam-Na, only half a dozen miles from the frontier, collect information on the region, prepare for our arrival in this sector and above all make contact with Dao Te-tiou, a powerful Thai chieftain whom we had known by repute for some time.

Fan came back at the end of a week. He seemed extremely pleased, not to say enthusiastic. Maybe he too had a passion for unknown territory? Maybe the Thai country and the 'savage races' were as intoxicating a philtre for him as the Burma Road had been for us? In any case, he seemed to have acquitted himself extremely well.* According to him, there

* I am now convinced he was infinitely sharper and more intelligent than we thought at the time, judging him as we did by Western standards and with our nerves strained to breaking point by Pin-Ku-Yin. I am also

was nothing to prevent us from transferring our headquarters to the neighbourhood of Muong-La. He had not been able to see Dao Te-tiou, since the latter was in prison as the result of a squabble with the local military. 'That man very bad,' he said, by which he meant the Thai leader was a dirty dog, which we knew already. According to all our information, Dao Te-tiou was an utter blackguard and ready to sell himself to the highest bidder. He was even suspected of passing information to the Japanese. But he came from a line of high mandarins, he wielded a great deal of influence and he was related to the great dignitaries of Tonkin. The very fact of his being venal might render him invaluable. That he was in prison just then detracted in no way from his prestige. A spell in jail was nothing unusual here: at Kunming it was not rare to see a colonel spend eight days in a cell, then resume his duties as though nothing had happened.

Be that as it may, though Dao Te-tiou was for the time being *hors de combat*, General An, who commanded the whole region and whom Fan had consulted by telephone, saw nothing against our move. He suggested of course an escort of soldiers to guard us and maintain our standing, which we were unable to refuse.

Fan had found us suitable quarters: a whole house, he said, with a room for each of us, not at Muong-La itself but in a fishing hamlet some distance away. He had been struck by the beauty of the region and complacently described it to us, mentioning also the amiability of the Thais, whom he still classified, however, under the heading of 'savage races'. He had also seen the messenger we had sent into Indo-China (the latter had been back for several days but had not bothered to come and report to us). This envoy had been unable to find any of our friends but had picked up the following information: at the moment there were no Japanese in the fourth

sure that if he too were one day to yield to the culpable temptation of writing his memoirs, Long and I would appear in them in just as curious a guise as the one in which he himself appears in these pages.

territory (the territory of Laichau). The French officer in command of this region was reputed to be hostile to them and was on friendly terms with the Chinese military leaders on the frontier. This sounded promising and we congratulated Fan on having brought his mission to a successful conclusion.

5

THE 'SAVAGE RACES'

Once the move had been decided upon, it took us only a few days to assemble mules and porters for the fifty-mile trip to Muong-La. We left Pin-Ku-Yin and its clouds without regret, after a farewell dinner with Colonel Song.

The going was less hard than on our previous journey. There was a proper path, leading continually downhill, first in a steep slope, then more gently, skirting the watercourse which gradually formed in the valley. We covered less than a third of the way on this first stage and stopped in a village on the banks of the river.

After our highland retreat, we had the impression of returning as though in a daze to the civilised world, in spite of the filth and exiguity of the village. There were houses with streets and shops which had dried fish, rice cakes and harsh black tobacco for sale. The sky was blue. The temperature came as a surprise. Accustomed to the rigours of the Pin-Ku-Yin climate, here we were in a muck sweat. No matter how much Fan protested, nothing could prevent us from swimming in the river.

We were received, needless to say, by the local military commander (there was not the smallest Yunnanese hamlet that did not possess a garrison and a commander). This one had not been here long and complacently described all his previous campaigns, at the same time insisting on showing us his wounds. He assured us that, if necessary, he would defend this corner of China to the death, and asked us, the next time we saw General Chiang Kai-shek, to assure him of his complete loyalty. Our reputation as great generals was beginning to be firmly established. We had our evening meal with the commander, a couple of notables and, much to our surprise, the local Communist delegate, who had based himself permanently on this little village and seemed to have a well-organised office and information centre.

We intended setting off again early in the morning, for a stage of about forty miles. But Fan did his utmost to detain us, using every possible excuse. First of all, it was the horses that were not ready; then their saddles couldn't be found; finally, one of the mules was sick. We were soon to learn the real reason for this delay: Fan had made up his mind to keep us well concealed. That was why he had found us quarters not at Muong-La itself but in an isolated hamlet. Now he wanted to make sure that we didn't go past Muong-La in broad daylight. It was rather childish, since our presence in Thai country was bound to be known.

We set off at last towards noon, in a tropical temperature. Luckily the track wasn't bad and we let the horses choose their own pace. As foreseen, we reached the outskirts of Muong-La after dark, towards ten in the evening. Fan was delighted. We were less so, having had nothing to eat since our departure. It began to rain and we were soon soaked to the skin, in spite of the broad-brimmed oilskin Chinese hats we had bought at the last stop and in which we must have cut fine figures.

Our stealthy progress past Muong-La is worth describing. There was a torrent-like stream just in front of the village. Fan, who had been over the road already, claimed he knew of a ford and undertook to lead the caravan across. He slithered down the bank and advanced confidently into the river-bed, signalling us to follow him, which we did as best we could in the pitch dark. Scarcely had his horse advanced two steps than he was up to his neck in water and in danger of being swept away. Maybe the level had risen since Fan was last here? In any case, the current was extremely strong and the ford impracticable. But Fan refused to acknowledge this obvious fact for fear of losing face and insisted on urging on his horse, which started to rear. The mules, which had seen what was happening, took fright and thrashed about in every direction, threatening to send our packs flying into the water. Fan cursed the drivers and struggled to get horses and mules across but the latter, which were more sensible, obstinately refused. The rain was coming down in sheets; the river was rising almost visibly. Exasperated all of a sudden by our colonel's pig-headedness, Long lost his temper and took command of the operation. Commonsense suggested making the whole caravan climb back up the slippery bank. This was easier said than done. It took us a whole hour, with the mules kicking, the muleteers yelling and almost having to carry each animal bodily, all of them utterly distracted by the roar of the torrent, the lightning and the flashlight which Fan, now at his wits' end, insisted on flashing in their faces.

When calm was restored to a certain degree, we noticed that this hullabaloo had attracted a crowd on the opposite bank. The entire population of Muong-La was assembled there, notified of our presence by the uproar. Such was the result of Fan's security measures!

But now reinforcements arrived. Some pirogues crossed the river and came to our assistance. After a moment's discussion it was clear that Fan had taken the wrong path: the ford was much further off. We scrambled into the vessels with our packs and saddles, while the unbridled horses swam across, guided by the expert hands of several villagers. It was thus, illuminated by rush torches which began to blaze one after another, that we eventually made our clandestine entry into Thai country.

The village headman, surrounded by notables, approached us with a conspiratorial air and whispered a few incomprehensible words in a low voice. We immediately gathered there was only one idea in their heads: to keep us concealed. Fan had driven the lesson home. Meanwhile the whole village was there, lurking in the shadows, so as not to miss a detail of our arrival!

It took us another two hours to reach the hamlet of Ti-Nah,* our final objective, but the rest of the journey was by pirogue. We abandoned the horses and also the packs, which we were to retrieve next day, and got into a long narrow vessel which the headman of Muong-La had made ready for his mysterious visitors. In pitch dark, in the pouring rain, our boatmen struggled against the current and sometimes stepped right into the water to drag the heavily laden pirogue through the rapids. We arrived at Ti-Nah towards three in the morning. Long and I had only one thought in our heads: to have a bite of food and go to bed. This of course was out of the question; the rice had to be cooked, the chicken had to be boiled, the water had to be heated. We waited in silence, feeling pleased in spite of everything at having arrived at the end of our journey, meanwhile drying ourselves in front of a fire which a thoughtful hand had lit on the earthen hearth in the middle of the house where we were to live.

The rites were eventually performed, the hot meal swallowed and washed down with copious draughts of rice spirit. The napkin dipped in boiling water was wiped across our dusty faces. We were now entitled to rest, under the protection of the Thai gods and four Chinese soldiers detailed to watch over our precious lives.

It was difficult to sleep in Thai country. The cocks saw fit to wake us at an unearthly hour and our new residence revealed itself to us in the early morning sunshine. It was an abrupt change of scene. There was nothing in common between the desolate rocks of Pin-Ku-Yin and this smiling valley crisscrossed with countless streams. The biggest was the Nam-Na, which watered Muong-La and on which we had travelled last night. The hamlet of Ti-Nah was surrounded by water on almost every side: in one direction by the Nam-Na, in another by one of its tributaries which described a semi-circle round the village. The valley was dominated by the mountains we had crossed.

* This is a made-up name; I have forgotten the real one.

106

The hamlet consisted of thirty or so houses, all made of bamboo, irregularly scattered among coconut and banana groves. Beyond the river there were some cultivated fields: rice, a little hemp and maize. Further on, thick green grass stretched all the way to the mountains and covered the nearest foothills.

Nor was there anything in common between the savage Chinese mountainfolk, whom we occasionally used to glimpse in the distance on the paths of Pin-Ku-Yin, and the natives among whom we were going to live. The Thais, who, some say, originally came down from Tibet to populate Siam, Laos, the valleys of Southern Yunnan and those of Upper Tonkin, were friendly, easy-going and amiable creatures. Like the Laotian, the Thai of Yunnan seems perfectly content with his fate provided he is able to eat a little rice, a little fish and, from time to time, a little pork. Those of Ti-Nah were no exception to this rule. They spent the whole day fishing or swimming in the river. They did not wear sarongs like the Laotians, but black Chinese trousers and smocks of the same colour. The women appeared to be slightly more industrious, and cultivated the maize and hemp fields. They were fairly pretty, but I found them less fine-featured than the Laotians. They wore black skirts and white blouses. It was only on feast days they appeared in multi-coloured sarongs, in which, however, black was always the dominant hue.

Our house was constructed entirely of bamboo. It was bigger, much cleaner than the Chinese huts and there were no rats. Built on stilts because of the damp, it consisted of a big central room with the hearth—merely a wooden case filled with earth and placed on the bamboo floor—a terrace with a veranda, which we decided to use as a dining room and, all the way round the central room, four smaller rooms to serve as bedrooms for Long, me, Mr Ho and Mr Ha. As for Fan, he had officially quartered himself on one of the locals—a woman, in fact. During his first visit he had made friends with an affable Thai lady and had now set up house with her without further ado. We were not displeased with this arrangement, which spared us from his perpetual and somewhat inopportune attentions.

We devoted the first morning to a tour of inspection. The Thais we met on our way smiled at us and didn't seem at all surprised to see us here. They are a philosophical people. The space between the piles under each house seethed with pigs and poultry. The former cleared up the garbage. Paradoxically, it was thanks to them that the hamlet was so clean. The cocks and the chickens were all cross-bred; wild cocks had looked in here.

Presently we noticed a hut situated at the far end of the hamlet where, on the terrace, a wizened old man sat motionless all day long beside an open coffin. We were told he was 'waiting for death'.

Thus we settled down to an organised life in Ti-Nah, a life that was infinitely more pleasant than at Pin-Ku-Yin but which soon, alas, proved to be just as monotonous. I would get up at seven in the morning and listen to the first bulletin from Radio Saigon. The news was always disappointing: brilliant Japanese successes announced with a great song and dance, followed by an advertisement for Copab cigarettes.

After that we did an hour's physical training on the banks of the river. Then one of us would go out with a rifle and shoot some pigeons in the flooded paddy fields. The other would sit down at a table and decode the latest signal from Chungking. Major T. seemed dissatisfied with the information we were sending him. The Chinese generals over there were convinced that the Japanese intended attacking Yunnan through the districts of Laichau and Laokay. Apparently they had likewise convinced T., who wanted us at all costs to report an intense activity in these regions. (Intelligence experts do sometimes indulge in these whims.) But this was absolutely contrary to the actual facts. The Japanese were not so crazy as to push into these mountains. In a fit of rage, Long summed up the situation in three questions: 'I wonder, in the first place, why the Japanese should want to conquer this country, secondly, why the Chinese should insist on defending it; thirdly, what the hell we are doing here.'*

Luncheon was served on the veranda, in company of Mr Ho, as stiff and inscrutable as ever, and Mr Ha, who sometimes did the cooking. As for Fan, he hardly ever left his young Thai lady. After lunch we would have a siesta, then go for a walk in the country, followed by a swim in the Nam-Na. And this would occupy us till dinnertime. Then, while our operators were fiddling with their sets, more often than not making contact with their girl friends in Chungking, Fan would put in an appearance. For form's sake we would ask him if there was any news from the other emissaries we had sent into Indo-China. He would reply in the negative and we would send him back to his Dulcinea. After which, fed up to the teeth, Mr Long and Mr Rule would sit out on the terrace overlooking the valley and exchange a few melancholy remarks about the odd war they were waging in this part of Asia.

Night would fall over the Nam-Na Valley. The highest mountains would vanish into the dark. The moon would rise above Yunnan and the cry of the river birds would break the silence. This was the time of day when the Thais emerged from their huts and gathered in a circle on the sand around a bamboo fire to ward off the damp, while the hamlet musician plucked at the strings of an odd-looking instrument which resembled no other intrument in the world, playing for hours on end the four self-same notes† of the single self-same tune. This meeting would go on as long as the moonlight lasted. If the moon was full, it would last all night.

The Thai women would spin their hemp, the young girls and children would dance round the fire. The elders, squatting on their haunches, would noisily smoke their water pipes, swig rice spirit and discuss the events of the day. The only absentee would be the old man who was 'waiting for death'.

* I'm not sure if this signal was ever dispatched. † I can still hear them.

He was obliterated by the dark but we could picture him in the shadows, motionless and silent beside his coffin.

Mr Long and Mr Rule, likewise shrouded in their isolation, would smoke the pungent local tobacco in their European pipes, their eyes fixed on the spluttering fire. Towards nine o'clock one of them would rouse himself from this beatitude to don ear-phones and tune in again to Radio Saigon: Radio Saigon, which would announce fresh Japanese successes and brag about them in a sickening manner. After the bulletin, a chorus consisting of the gilded French youth of Indo-China and a few enlisted Annamite children would assure the head of the French State, to the accompaniment of a barrel organ, that they were 'Ready and Prepared to Do Their Duty'. Finally, a snivelling southern voice would give vent to a further spate of the lies that had done us so much harm, consigning to the scaffold such traitors as Mr Long and Mr Rule, and end up by comparing an eighty-year-old dodderer with that young virgin who turfed the enemy out of France a great many years before.

At ten o'clock we would rouse ourselves again, this time to listen to Radio Chungking in English. On this station the announcer was a Chinese, who tried so hard to assume an American accent that he was almost incomprehensible. He would describe the latest celestial successes and enumerate the number of Japanese divisions that had been wiped out in the course of the last few days.

Meanwhile the Thai family party would be going on just outside in the moonlight. The musician would continue to strum his four notes, over and over again, the children would continue to dance round the fire and throw twigs into the flames, the elders would continue to drink, the adults to do nothing, and the old man on the terrace would continue to wait for death beside his coffin.

A depressing period. I sadly reflected I had done nothing but move from one place to another ever since the outbreak of the war, travelling round a large circumference whose centre was situated somewhere in Siam: Annam, Cochin-China, Singapore, Rangoon, the Burma Road, Kunming, Pin-Ku-Yin, Muong-La. And here I was back again at the gates of Indo-China. Only a few steps were needed to complete the circle. I had had some splendid trips, known the joy of potential adventure, the elating experience of setting out on a hazardous expedition; and it looked as though a mischievous god was doing his utmost to transform our escapade into a tourist excursion punctuated by Chinese meals. Once again nothing came of our efforts. We failed to re-establish contact with our friends over the border. There were too many Chinese intermediaries between us and them, too many interpreters, too many gestures of courtesy. Or maybe we just didn't know how to set about it?

Our hopes revived a little when we had a visit from Dao Te-tiou. He had come out of prison at last and, of his own accord, manifested the wish to meet us. He arrived at our house, after crossing the numerous stretches of water surrounding it, and deigned to have a meal with us.

He was a degenerate warlord with thin, unkempt hair. Fan, who did not like him, kept repeating: 'He very bad man.' But, as we expected, in spite of his spell in prison his prestige with the Thais was immense. The head of our hamlet showed him even more respect than he did to Long and me. Dao Te-tiou haughtily accepted it. The fact was he inspired mortal terror in all the petty officials. He had a number of partisans on his pay-roll and levied taxes according to his needs. He would live like this for a long time, rich and feared, unless he vanished mysteriously one day after being summoned by some great general, or a shot fired from behind a bush put an end to his career ... The Thais were a gentle, easy-going people who liked fishing in the river and congregating peacefully in the moonlight, did I say? This remained to be seen. At all events, they sometimes lost their tempers. I even began to wonder if my idyllic first impression of them did not conceal some completely different reality.

I was no longer sure of anything. Fan had told us the
reason why the dwellings of the great and smaller chiefs were
hermetically closed here, why the rooms in which they usually
lived had no windows. It was to make sure that no shot could
be fired or a spear flung from outside. Something else had contributed to my doubts: for some time we had noticed an
innocent-looking Thai who followed the hamlet headman
everywhere like a shadow and lavished an almost filial solici-
tude on him. The other day we saw him undress before diving
into the river to free his pirogue, which was wedged between a
couple of tree trunks. Under his black smock, next to his bare
skin, he wore an arsenal that would have done justice to a
pirate: a modern sub-machine gun, a pistol, a dagger and two
hand grenades.

Dao Te-tiou himself never moved without an escort of five
or six partisans armed with muskets. These men kept guard
outside the door whenever he had a meal with us, and scrutin-
ised each of his guests in a most unpleasant manner.

'He decidedly very bad man.' After one of these meals Long
asked for his help, dangling the prospect of gain in front of his
eyes. He looked interested and promised us his support.
Treachery was always possible with someone of this sort, but
he was frightened of the Chinese military, whose powers now
outstripped his own. We hoped he would toe the line, being
torn between love of money and the fear of a fresh spell in
prison. Thanks to him, we would now be able to infiltrate some
more agents into Indo-China.

A feast was organised that evening in honour of his visit by
the hamlet of Ti-Nah. The women and young girls donned
their ceremonial sarongs and performed a series of dances in
honour of the great Thai warlord.

June, 1942

There had been some changes in the mission. May had
packed up and left China. He had been replaced in Kunming
by Léonard, whom T. had transferred from Chungking.

Léonard's first move was to imprison Colonel Cha, who had apparently been indulging in a shameless misappropriation of the supplies intended for us. At last we received the cigarettes and money we had been requesting for so long, plus a tin of English tobacco and a bottle of whisky, which came as a pleasant surprise.

Léonard must have clearly understood our state of mind from the tone of our latest signals and was now doing his best to look after our morale as well as our physical welfare. His consignment contained a bundle of English newspapers and French periodicals which he had unearthed in Kunming. They were mostly back numbers of *Illustration*. It would be difficult for anyone to imagine the avidity with which we devoured them. Only someone who has lived as we had been living for several months would be able to understand the pleasure that could be derived from a back number of *Illustration*. Since our departure from Kunming, our only reading matter had been two books which we perused almost every day, two books in English on which our code was based: *Turnabout* by Thorne Smith and *The Hound of the Baskervilles* by Conan Doyle.*

Finally, Léonard sent us a long summary of the local news, including the following items: fighting had broken out recently on the Kunming aerodrome between the troops of the Central Government and those of the province, the governor of which was still under suspicion. The scuffle grew into a pitched battle, with an exchange of rifle shots and bursts of machine-gun fire throughout the day. Chiang Kai-shek's troops had eventually got the better of it, but there had been some fatal casualties and a number of wounded on both sides.

The information gleaned on F., the French commander of Laichau District, was more and more encouraging. He had apparently voiced his sympathy for the Allies on several occasions and declared that the Japanese would never set foot in

* I can still recite whole passages from them by heart.

his district as long as he was there. We decided to try to establish contact with him. Without revealing our presence here, we
sent him word that a Chinese officer of the Central Government (this would be Fan) would like to have a meeting with
him on the frontier. He replied that he agreed to this and suggested as a rendezvous the French military post of Ba Na-
koum. This post was situated a hundred yards from the border,
facing a Chinese village of the same name.

Meanwhile we decided to go and inspect this famous frontier, to which we were gradually drawing closer, and study on
the spot the possibilities of crossing it. We were beginning to
realise we would never get anything done unless we entered
Indo-China ourselves.

There was no difficulty about getting to Ba Na-koum. (Getting back, however, was another matter.) We merely had to set
off in a pirogue and drift down-stream. We first descended the
little river watering Ti-Nah; then the Nam-Na, which had a
strong current. The women washing at the river showed
no surprise as we glided past. Our presence must have been
known to all and sundry. The Nam-Na, which was fairly
broad at Muong-La, presently grew narrower, flowing betwen
sheer cliffs. We negotiated several rapids and arrived at Ba
Na-koum in about an hour and a half.

The village headman was a splendid type of Thai, with
long whiskers which made him look rather like an old-time
corsair. He invited us to the inevitable meal before allowing
us to talk business. Ba Na-koum was a poor village but it did us
proud. There was course after course, an abundance to which
we were unaccustomed. The stodgy mountain rice was served
in little wicker baskets, from which each of us took a handful.

The village headman had a pleasant manner. He spoke
little, preferring to knock off glass after glass of rice spirit
between each course while contemplating his guests. Presently,
in the penumbra of the hut, his eyes began to sparkle above
his pirate's whiskers. 'He is a friend after our own heart,'

Long declared, quoting a sentence of Sherlock Holmes's from *The Hound of the Baskervilles*, which we knew by heart.

Fan, who had started to speak a few words of Thai,* tried to strike up a conversation with him.

The French post opposite the village was commanded by a Lieutenant P., who had a nasty reputation among the Thais and Chinese. 'He very bad man,' was the opinion of our colonel interpreter, whose vocabulary was not very extensive. This confirmed our previous information. It was therefore essential that he should not discover our true identity, even if he heard of the arrival of two Europeans at Ba Na-koum, which seemed impossible to avoid. Except to a few initiates in the secret of the gods, it was more and more important that we should appear as British subjects attached as advisers to the Chinese Government.

After the meal we crossed the river in a pirogue and, escorted by a guide from the village, under cover of the undergrowth, made our way to the frontier. There it was: a few paces off lay French Indo-China, a land that had haunted our dreams for many a month. We could see the post, less than a hundred yards away, separated from us by a little stream marking the boundary between the two countries. It was a concrete post, with white walls and a red-tiled roof, which looked like a palace compared to the huts to which we were accustomed.

The French flag fluttered above the building. Annamite riflemen stood on guard. We saw an officer, no doubt Lieutenant P., strolling up and down a veranda. A bugle sounded; it was dinnertime. I heard a thousand familiar sounds which reminded me of my sojourn in Indo-China. We remained there for some time, lost in contemplation. Finally, without being observed, we returned, silent and pensive, towards our allies of the moment, the Chinese and the Thais.

We broached the burning question with the village headman: which were the possible paths to enter Indo-China

* Thanks to his sleeping dictionary.

clandestinely? It was not easy to get a word out of the old fox, who was well aware of our intention but who had no wish to give away the secrets of his fellow smugglers to strangers. Little by little, however, after urging him to drink a few more glasses of rice spirit, we obtained some fairly interesting information, in particular on the navigability of the rivers, a question which had begun to obsess me.

We mustn't dream, he told us, of descending the Nam-Na from Ba Na-koum. P.'s riflemen kept a close watch day and night. Furthermore, shortly after the post, there was a waterfall several yards high which no vessel could negotiate. After this obstacle, however, the river was more or less navigable, at certain times of the year, by light pirogues. It was not impossible, he concluded, to cross the frontier on foot, at night, and reach the Nam-Na down-stream from the waterfall. But then we would have to find a vessel there . . . unless we transported one across the mountains, which could also be managed at a pinch.

After the evening meal, at which the Thai really astounded us by the amount of alcohol he continued to consume without turning a hair, we lay down in his house on some dusty bunks. The hut was hermetically sealed, of course, and I didn't sleep a wink all night. I kept thinking of P., the river, the waterfall, and working out various means of overcoming these obstacles. I could hear Long tossing and turning under his mosquito net, no doubt obsessed by the same thoughts.

We returned to Ti-Nah the next day. We had taken an hour and a half to come down the river. It took us six hours to get back. The corsair with the whiskers had chosen the longest and heaviest pirogue he could find for us, no doubt as a mark of distinction, and the boatmen had to exert themselves to their utmost.

Apart from his duties as an interpreter, Fan was engaging with a conspiratorial air in mysterious activities with which his masters in Chungking had no doubt entrusted him, unbeknown to us. He spread the good word around, the good

116

word of General Chiang Kai-shek. He was extremely popular
with the locals and had founded a so-called 'Youth Organisation' for the adolescents and infants of the village. The
children swore loyalty to the master of China (and also, I
believe, to his prophet Fan), sang patriotic songs and held
top-secret meetings at which the colonel presided. He told us
his organisation would gradually spread as far as the frontier,
extend into Indo-China and reach Hanoi, where it would
render invaluable service. Unfortunately, we could not be sure
that the aim of this fraternity was to render invaluable service
to us.

Moreover, each member of this organisation was a budding
counter-espionage agent. Fan, who was now obsessed by
security, kept seeing enemies round every corner. He came to
us after dinner one evening and told us a sinister story: an old
man who lived alone in an isolated shanty some distance from
the village had been observed prowling round our house. He
had tried to gather information about us from the children and
had then been seen heading for the forest in the direction of
the frontier. Our colonel was convinced the man was a spy,
which was not altogether unlikely.

Fan alerted his youth members and the little fishing village
was transformed into a camp of conspirators. The old man
apparently wore spectacles and never moved without his
umbrella. It would have been unhealthy for a seventy-year-old
stranger to wander round Ti-Nah at night equipped with these
accessories. Every Thai in the place (the adults having joined
the youth organisation) was now haunted by the spectre of an
old man with an umbrella and spectacles. After dark the
silence of the torch-lit circle would be broken by conspiratorial
whispers, while every eye would be turned towards our house.
We could no longer move a yard without being followed by
apprentice detectives intent on protecting us, come what may.
Fan begged us not to go out at night without being escorted by
two armed soldiers. The trouble was, we could never find out if
he was genuinely apprehensive or whether he had merely made

up the story just to have an additional excuse for keeping us hidden away.

An interlude: the wild boar had come down from the mountains and were causing havoc in the maize fields. We spent a few evenings lying in wait for them but always came back empty-handed. The only time I came across a group of them, about ten strong, was one evening when, for a wonder, I was out without a rifle. While we cut sorry figures as hunters, Fan covered himself in glory one night by bagging a magnificent solitary with a single musket shot. The whole village woke up at once and filed past the animal. Pandemonium broke loose. Mr Ho, the townsman, shed his habitual reserve and danced with delight. The excitement lasted until morning, for the Thais hardly ever seemed to sleep and would seize any opportunity to spend the night chatting and swigging alcohol.

Another diversion: illness. I had an attack of dysentery from which I only half recovered, and on top of that a dose of malaria which kept me in bed two days. Fan also went down with a bout of malaria. We went and saw him in his girl friend's house, where he was treated by having cups of scalding tea poured down his throat all day long.

Mr Ha, the younger of our two operators, caused us greater anxiety. One night he started writhing on his bunk in the throes of a violent colic. Fan assured us it was cholera, a common disease in the district. Mr Ha was seized by ghastly convulsions. Four of us together were unable to prevent him from toppling out of bed. He then went on writhing on the floor, frothing at the mouth, twisting his limbs and shrieking. And, in addition to the pain, the poor wretch had to endure the Chinese treatment inflicted on him unanimously by his colleague Mr Ho, Fan and the village doctor who had been called into consultation. I never saw anything like it: the poor fellow was slapped, pummelled, clawed, then beaten to a pulp by his doctors. We dared not intervene; maybe it was the proper treatment after all. And indeed Mr Ha got up next morning bright and cheerful, apparently oblivious

of the fact that he had been moribund the night before.
He gobbled up our last tin of bully beef to round off his
recovery.

We had a second meeting with Dao Te-tiou, who had
heard about our visit to the frontier and was more and more
interested in our plans. This time he invited us to his domain
not far from Muong-La. There we also met a younger brother
of his who was married to an Annamite woman and spoke
quite good French.

Dao Te-tiou lived in a curious house which still bore some
traces of his family's former splendour but which he had
allowed to go to ruin. It was approached through a double
enclosure of stone walls, which had once been whitewashed
but which in their present filthy state echoed the decline of
the proprietor. The furniture, which must have been comfortable, was now dilapidated. The walls were hung with por-
traits of his ancestors, who looked most impressive. I was
reminded of the House of Usher.

We were determined not to beat about the bush. Long
offered him a large sum in exchange for his support and asked
him, as a start, to put us in touch with a certain Chinese
merchant in Laichau who was utterly devoted to him and
would be a valuable ally to us. Tomorrow and not a day later
he was to arrange for this merchant to meet us somewhere on
the frontier.

The negotiations were accompanied by lengthy professions
of friendship and disinterestedness on his part, conveyed by
his brother, who elaborated on them, I thought, and who
struck me as being as much of a blackguard as his elder. Then
came a long complaint about times being hard, bad harvests
and the hostility of the military who had caused him heavy
financial losses. We reassured him we knew how to recognise
his services. The session was rounded off by a number of toasts
exchanged to the health of all the Allies.

We made our way back to Ti-Nah across the paddy fields,
escorted, in addition to our usual guard, by some partisans

whom the Thai warlord had insisted on lending us as a mark of distinction.

July, 1942

Another expedition to Ba Na-koum. The date fixed by Major F. for his meeting with a Chinese officer had arrived. We were anxious to attend it. Furthermore, after many a hesitation, Long had decided to reveal our presence to F. and ask for a personal interview, using Fan as an intermediary.

Having arrived on the eve of the appointed day, we spent the night in the hut of the corsair with the bristling whiskers. It looked as though we had reached a turning point in our odyssey. If F. agreed to meet us and help us (not a vain hope, according to all the information we had received on him) it would be a trump card in our hand for communication with Indo-China. If he refused, he would probably report our presence to the powers that be and our enterprise would be sadly jeopardised.*

The meeting was to take place at midday. Fan was extremely nervous. He had donned his best uniform and put on the badges of rank of a general. We spent the whole morning briefing him, and Long handed him a letter addressed to Major F., a letter signed in his real name, reporting as an officer of Free France and requesting an interview. Needless to say, this message was to be delivered unbeknown to Lieutenant P.

Our interpreter returned blushing with pride and with a triumphant expression, after being asked to stay for lunch at the French post. This was his report: F. had been charming ('A very pretty man,' he told us.) They had drunk copiously to the success of the Chinese armies and the major had reasserted that he loathed the Japanese. He had read Long's letter

* After being confined for months in a closed circle, our minds had reached the stage at which finer shades are eliminated. We could envisage nothing except For or Against, forgetting the infinite variety of intermediary tones, which are the more common lot of mankind.

with great attention. Then he had thought it over and told Fan he would gladly meet us but not today, since he was busy and had to get back to Laichau at once. He had promised to arrange a meeting with us in four or five days' time at the latest.

I let myself be carried away by Fan's optimism. Judging by what he said, the Allied cause had no more fervent partisan than Major F. More prudently, Long expressed his astonishment that he was unable to come and see us that day, if he was really so anxious to do so. But there may have been many reasons to prevent him, not least the proximity of P. We regarded this promise as an initial success and celebrated it that evening in the hut of the corsair with the whiskers.

On our return to Muong-La next morning, we waited in a fever of excitement for four days, five days, one week, two weeks. Still no news. We were now far less optimistic. On second thoughts, hadn't we been rather naïve? What would a seasoned and well-disciplined officer do on receiving a message such as ours? It was a safe bet that he would make a report to his superiors . . . who would do likewise, and so on up to top level. Since we were labouring under no illusion as to how we were regarded by the higher military and civilian spheres in Indo-China, the help we were expecting was liable to turn into a fierce opposition and merciless tussle.

What was happening over there was now out of our hands. Yet never had we felt such longing and need for action. After considering the situation from every angle and weighing all the chances, we finally reverted to my famous plan: to descend the Nam-Na on a vessel of some sort, thus reach the Black River, then the Red River, and end up at Hanoi, where I would find friends to help and protect me.

I pestered Long every day to allow me to make the attempt. He had detected the hazardous, not to say crazy aspect of the scheme from the very start, but I had succeeded so well in convincing myself it was the most reasonable thing in the world that I gradually managed to win him over. Thereupon he decided to come with me. Evening after evening we thrashed out the details of this adventure, which no longer appeared as a romantic dream but a specific plan which would be carried out in the near future.

A sensational development altered our schemes. Major T. forwarded us a signal from the Committee in London: remembering all of a sudden what Long had done for Free France since 1940, the Committee was asking for his immediate recall to take up a senior appointment. T. advised him to accept.

Long hesitated for a long time. On the one hand, we neither of us deceived ourselves as to how slender our chances of success were in Indo-China at the moment. He had no doubt that he could be more usefully employed elsewhere than in this country of 'savage races'. On the other, I could see that he did not want to abandon an enterprise which had been his own brain child and which he had supported from the very beginning. Furthermore, he knew that I was not going to give up the expedition and he hated to see me go off on my own. We thrashed the matter out for the whole of one day and one night. I advised him to accept the offer he had been made. He still couldn't make a decision. He sent a signal to be forwarded to London saying that he was mobilised and was therefore awaiting orders. At the same time we informed Major T. of my plan to get to Hanoi by river.

Since we still received no word from F., we could no longer count on that trump card. In the end I managed to get Long's permission to make the attempt on my own.

The Descent of the Nam-Na

THE RAFT

From the moment the expedition was decided upon until the time of my departure, I had no other thought in my head. I lived in a state of morbid excitement, alternating between crazy speculations on the possible hazards and feverish work on the minutest details. For a long time, far longer than I have indicated here, I had been dreaming more or less consciously of entering Indo-China by some such means. At Singapore, long before the Japanese invasion, I had already envisaged a similar scheme, starting from Siam (since we were on good terms with the Siamese), descending one of the tributaries of the Mekong, then the Mekong itself, and ending up in Cambodia. The memory of canoe trips on rivers in France was not unconnected with my perseverance with these plans. I had had some experience of rivers (and I pride myself on having even more now!). I knew how treacherous they could be with their eddies, their cross-currents, their abrupt bends followed by seething rapids between sheer cliffs. I now felt I had been born to bring this enterprise to a successful conclusion. I also felt that only a madman would fail to use such a heaven-sent method. The rivers poured their waters into Indo-China every second; I merely had to drift down with the current.

I merely had to . . . The first consideration was the choice of a vessel. Pirogues and sampans were out of the question, since I had to cross the frontier on foot and march through the night before embarking. A small canoe, on the other hand, would not stand up to the rapids. I merely had to . . . I was seized with such frenzy that for several days my head buzzed with the most fantastic schemes. I seriously thought of swimming down the river, supporting myself on a plank—an admirable plan, had it been a question of only a few miles, but it was two or three hundred from here to Hanoi.

Long refused to discuss this project, but, with his usual enthusiasm for practical experiment, forced me to put it to the test. And so, on a moonless night (my voyage had to be undertaken in the dark) we both waded into the water at Ti-Nah (for he insisted on seeing for himself) and let ourselves be carried down-stream as far as Muong-La, escorted by a boat piloted by the faithful Fan, who that evening must have entertained serious doubts as to our mental equilibrium. It took us about twenty minutes to reach our objective, but long before this we were numb, almost paralysed by the cold. We could not have kept going much longer. I felt rather sheepish. Long said nothing, but this icy dip brought me to my senses and I tried to think of some other solution to the problem.

Eureka! I decided to build a light raft from the big bamboos that grew in abundance on the outskirts of the village. This raft was to be just large enough to carry me and my stores, and would have to be collapsible so that I could carry it across the mountains to my embarkation point.

Long, who was somewhat skeptical of my inventions since our nocturnal swim, insisted on seeing the raft before expressing an opinion. Meanwhile he sent a signal to Léonard, asking him if it was possible to find a rubber canoe in Kunming similar to those used by American airmen. I added a long list of various bits of equipment which were not available here, in particular, waterproof sheeting and thin cord. Léonard replied that he was doing his utmost to get me the material and to send it to us by the next runner.

We received a signal from T., who was alarmed at the very idea of the expedition and advised against it, albeit without giving it his veto. I was furious when I read this message an my first reaction was to reply in somewhat disrespectful terr Nevertheless, we still held our position.

A third trip to Ba Na-koum. We had to reconnoitre the ground for the frontier crossing and also meet the Chinese merchant from Laichau, Dao Te-tiou's friend, a certain Song-Seng, who had agreed to work with us and was to maintain liaison between the interior and the exterior. We went, as usual, by pirogue. I noticed the Nam-Na had risen considerably: it was now a raging torrent. The boatmen had difficulty in keeping the vessel steady in the swirl and preventing it from smashing against the rocks. Throughout the descent I sat deep in thought. I kept picturing myself on my raft, *en route* to Hanoi.

Dao Te-tiou and his brother, who insisted on attending the meeting, were waiting for us at Ba Na-koum. Horses had been provided for us. We set off for the meeting place, guided by the whiskered chieftain who had likewise joined the expedition. The appointed spot was three hours away. As we left the village we crossed some paddy fields in full view of the French post. No one, however, appeared to take any notice of us. We scrambled up the mountain overlooking the right bank of the Nam-Na and came out onto a sort of plateau above the valley. Leaving the horses in the care of some partisans, we advanced on foot down to the river bed forming the boundary between China and Indo-China. Then, climbing uphill again on the other side, we reached an isolated hamlet on the top of a mountain. It was a Houni village. I immediately felt at home again among these black-clad men. A village? A lair, rather. The only regular occupation here was smuggling. The whiskered Thai told me I would have to start from here to cross the frontier. The Hounis would act as guides and porters.

Song-Seng would not be here for another hour. The Houni chieftain in his turn did us the honours of his hut. He gave me to understand without further ado that he would like to smoke my pipe. I hastened to hand it to him.

We talked about the frontier crossing. It was a difficult conversation: every question we asked had to be translated from French into Chinese, from Chinese into Thai and from Thai

into Houni. We managed to come to an understanding, however. At least I hoped so.

The Houni chief would put five men at my disposal, a guide
and four porters. They would be responsible for getting me
across the frontier secretly and guiding me, after a night's
march over the mountains, to a tributary of the Nam-Na, at
which point I would merely have to embark on my raft for a
destination which was no concern of theirs. The price was
settled. We fixed the departure date for August 1st. This long
and laborious discussion among Frenchmen, Chinese, Thais
and Hounis took place in a dark and hermetically sealed hut.
The Hounis were adopting the same security measures as the
other natives.

Song-Seng turned up at last, creeping out of the Indo-
Chinese undergrowth. He looked like a well-to-do Chinese,
quick-witted and not overburdened by scruples. He was likewise accompanied by a relative, a brother-in-law or cousin.
The Chinese have a strong family sense. Both of them were
dressed in brand-new shorts, shirts and khaki stockings. It was
the same colonial uniform as I used to wear out there, minus
badges of rank and regimental insignia.

Song-Seng and his cousin spoke French with curious Annamite intonations, which should have made the discussion
easier. But Fan seemed particularly keen on keeping Chinese as
the diplomatic language, so that Dao Te-tiou and the Hounis
also joined in, each in his own idiom. We finally understood
what it was all about. Whereas we were obsessed by the prospect of the expedition and the need to maintain a link between
Hanoi and the frontier, our friends had primarily been
impressed by the quality of the cloth in which their brothers
from Indo-China were dressed. The remarks that had been
exchanged under our noses for the last ten minutes were aimed
merely at working out a deal in contraband cloth between
Tonkin and Yunnan!

Long authoritatively brought the conversation back to the
subject of the day. Song-Seng agreed to establish the link. He

had great facilities for moving about in Indo-China. I told him I intended making for Hanoi by a secret route (there was no reason to tell him more) and arranged to meet him there after August 10th—as though I had already arrived!

All that remained to be arranged was the question of the remuneration, which did not take long. The Chinese left us, wishing me a pleasant journey. We felt it had been a good day on the whole and that things were looking up. We immediately showed our gratitude to Dao Te-tiou by handing over a fairly substantial sum which would enable him to pay his taxes to the authorities. We then set off on the return journey, after a final look at the mountains of Indo-China.

Shortly afterwards our Yunnanese runner arrived from Kunming, bringing Léonard's best wishes, a bottle of whisky and a few implements I had requested. Our friend Léonard must have had some difficulty in collecting this equipment so quickly. The only thing missing was the rubber canoe, which was not available at Kunming. The die was cast: it would have to be the raft.

There was just enough time for me to make my preparations. I started off by plotting my course on a large-scale map: the Nam-Na Valley, the Black River and the Red River, by way of Laichau, Sonla and Hoa-Binh. I memorised the important points, especially the tributaries, which would act as sign posts, the villages and the stretches where the contour lines suggested rapids. Estimating the speed of the current, I hoped to reach Hanoi in six days, or rather six nights, for I would have to lie up in the forest during the day-time.

My luggage would consist of two bundles: the first would be a suitcase wrapped in waterproof sheeting, containing whatever I would need on my arrival at Hanoi, that is to say, a civilian suit, some money and various documents, including letters of introduction to some friends. To these I added a list of the bridges and engineering works on the Hanoi–Saigon railway line, a manual on modern methods of sabotage and five copies of a French-Chinese glossary which would serve as a code.

The second, containing supplies for the voyage, would consist of an inner tube, cut in two, which I had asked Léonard to send me. All this would be firmly lashed to the raft.

The raft was the most important piece of equipment and I set to work on it without further delay. Fan mobilised his entire youth movement to collect an impressive pile of hollow bamboos with a diameter of about three inches. After several trials which proved unsatisfactory I adopted the following plan: my raft would be built in two halves cut lengthways, each half consisting of two superimposed rows of bamboos. A space between each layer would enable a crossbar to be inserted to adjust the two sections. Each of these would be about twelve inches wide. Between the two I would leave an empty space, likewise twelve inches wide, so as to increase the total width and stability. I would sit on a plank placed crosswise, with my legs stretched along the bamboos or else in the water.

I worked frantically for several days before obtaining a decent result. I insisted on doing everything myself and refused any help from the Thais. I could think of nothing but this raft: I dreamt about it at night. I was well aware it would be subjected to a severe strain and I took care to see that the bamboos formed a solid block capable of withstanding fairly violent jolts. I tore the skin off my hands binding and knotting the Chinese rope which Léonard had sent me, the only kind he had been able to find in Kunming, which bristled with prickles as sharp as needles. Long offered to help me, but I now regarded this venture as my personal affair and insisted on settling even the smallest details on my own.

The contraption was eventually finished. All that remained was to try it out. With bated breath I launched it, under the amused and awed gaze of the Thais. The raft kept afloat, which was the main thing, although my position was rather uncomfortable. In fact, I found myself sitting right in the water, but that was better than being up to one's neck in it. Furthermore, my vessel was practically unmaneuverable on account of its square shape. Using a long bamboo as a paddle,

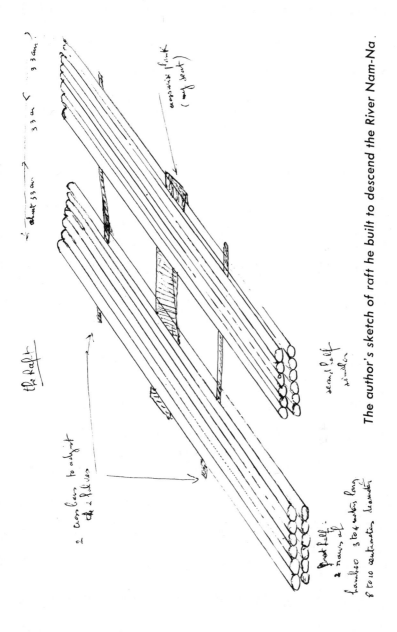

The author's sketch of raft he built to descend the River Nam-Na.

I could just keep it parallel to the current, but that was about all. But was there any need for me to maneuver? All I had to do was drift down to Hanoi. Besides, it had an enormous advantage in my eyes. It was light and could be taken to pieces easily. Each of the two sections weighed no more than fifty pounds. I was familiar enough with the Hounis to know that this burden wouldn't daunt them.

I convinced myself this was just the contraption I needed to succeed. For two pins I would have boasted that I had created a work of art. I had the first undisturbed night I had known for several weeks.

The appointed date was approaching. I now devoted all my attention to the baggage. I had to make everything completely watertight, for I foresaw, and with reason, that I would frequently be submerged and I had no wish to end up at Hanoi with a soaking-wet suit. Fortunately Léonard had been anything but stingy and there was plenty of waterproof sheeting. I wrapped my suitcase in several layers, stuck together, and finished off the edges with sealing wax. Finally I bisected my inner tube and stuffed the supplies for the voyage into the two halves: cooked rice, grilled beef, sugar and a bottle of Chinese rice wine. I joined the two ends and, by squeezing these between two bits of wood fastened with elastic bands, I obtained a fairly watertight join, which I prided myself on having invented.

I then tested the complete cargo in the river. The suitcase was lashed to the prow of the raft. The inner tube, arranged in a crescent behind me, served as a backrest. The whole thing looked rather strange but it kept afloat and the luggage did not let in any water.

The time had come to leave Muong-La and the valley. I spent my last day resting. Fan asked me for a personal interview. He professed his devotion over and over again and ended up by assuring me that he was very fond of me. I didn't question his sincerity and at that moment, I believe, I entertained the same feelings towards him. Mr Ho and Mr

Ha likewise bade me an emotional farewell. We spent the last evening, Long and I, sitting out on the veranda overlooking the circle of Thai villagers conversing in undertones in the dark. The musician was not playing that night.

We set off for Ba Na-koum well before daybreak. I naturally took this opportunity to make a serious and extensive trial. I drifted down-stream on my fully laden raft, escorted by Long and Fan in a pirogue. The vessel behaved reasonably well except, as I said, that it was more or less unsteerable.* After a sudden bend in the river I was flung against the bank and dragged on to the rocks through the trees without being able to control it. I managed all the same to extricate myself and arrived at Ba Na-koum without further mishap. My bundles and dismantled raft were laden onto some mules and we headed for the Houni village which was my point of departure. We reached it in the morning.

The porters and the guide were there. All that remained was to wait for the dark. We spent the day in the hut of the chieftain, who kept peering at me with curiosity. We were all strangely silent. After this period of excitement I was anxious to be on my own at last, and up and doing. The last hours seemed endless.

Nevertheless we had a long talk in the afternoon with the Houni guide. Long wanted to make sure that our countless interpreters had briefed him properly and that he had understood what he had been told. Fan assured us that everything was perfect.

* I reproached myself bitterly later on, and still reproach myself today, for not having used bamboos of a different size, longer ones in the centre, so as to give it a pointed instead of a rectangular shape. Alas, I had no leisure at the time to ponder on the imperatives of the mechanics of fluids !

2

THE NAM-NA

August, 1942

Every incident of this strange voyage is so deeply engraved on
my memory, and I have subsequently recalled it so often, that
I can describe it day by day, hour by hour, minute by minute.

First night

I started off at sunset. At the last moment Fan presented me
with a locally manufactured knife. I promised to bring him
back a revolver when I returned. I assured Long for the last
time that I felt perfectly confident and we parted with emotion. This time tomorrow I would be on my own in the Indo-
Chinese bush.

It started raining as soon as I set off. I crossed the frontier
in the last glimmer of daylight and immediately afterwards
there was an incident, not a serious one but a portent of what
was to come. My Houni guide, who was leading the expedition, suddenly stopped dead, motioned me to wait and, with
an anxious expression, pointed in the direction from which
we had come. I didn't understand what he meant, but did as
he said. While the porters pushed ahead in the dark, the two
of us remained standing in the rain for five minutes, ten
minutes, a quarter of an hour. My guide began to look impatient and kept waving his arms and gabbling away. In the
end I realised: he was waiting for the second man, he was
waiting for Long! He hadn't understood a word of Fan's
briefing! I managed to tell him in sign language that the
other foreigner was staying behind, and we set off again in the

wake of the porters; but I was somewhat anxious about the outcome of the expedition after this demonstration of the clarity of the briefing he had been given.

I have already described my admiration for the Hounis and the way in which they carried incredible loads along the most outrageous paths. They were to astonish me yet again before I took leave of their country. During the night on which I crossed the Indo-Chinese border they made me follow a route that defied the imagination. We negotiated precipices, scrambled up sheer cliffs, hacked our way through undergrowth which even the wild boar avoided. We crept along river beds over which the bush had spread an inextricable tangle of briars. I wasn't carrying anything, I was used to mountain climbing, yet I wasn't able to keep up with them. My Houni friends, the 'savage races', covered this ground with all my equipment on their backs, not to mention the raft, a cumbersome load if ever there was one, albeit not so heavy, which got entangled in every branch.

As soon as we entered the forest I was completely blind and had to use my flashlight; not for long, for it was put out of action by the rain and the spray from the torrents which soaked us to the skin. I stumbled along in darkness that can be imagined only by those who have spent a stormy night in the middle of an equatorial forest. I had to keep one hand on the shoulder of the Houni walking in front of me, invisible and soundless—so soundless that I had to call out whenever I happened to let go of him for a couple of seconds.

After an hour's march the sandals I had put on so as to be more nimble came to pieces and I lost them in the water. There was no question of stopping to look for them and I went on barefoot, over razor-sharp rocks and lacerating grass, without wasting time on recrimination.

We climbed up-hill for several hours. I kept thinking of the glorious moment when I would be able at last to settle down on my raft and merely drift along with the current. Eventually we reached a plateau where the forest was less dense and followed a narrow track. My feet were in a woeful condition. Putting my hands to my calves, I felt several bloated leeches adhering in a slimy mass to a coating of mud and congealed blood.

The rain stopped at last. It grew less dark and I could see the outline of the black-clad men in front of me. The hardest part was over. We were deep in the interior of Indo-China and were now skirting some cultivated fields. It was about one in the morning.

The outline of a village loomed up in the darkness which was gradually dissolving. The guide suddenly seized me by the arm, making me lie down. A flashlight had gleamed over there through the trees. We waited for several minutes, which seemed an eternity to me, but the flashlight drew further and further away and finally vanished in the forest. Some nocturnal hunter, no doubt, trying to trap the eyes of a passing deer in the beam of his lamp, or else a smuggler who, like us, preferred to avoid an encounter.

The remainder of the march was along a real track. Towards three in the morning, after a fairly steep descent into a valley, we reached the bank of a stream which was no more than four or five feet wide and seemed half clogged with tall grass and boulders. Triumphantly the Houni guide gave me to understand that we had reached our objective. So this was the result of the detailed instructions given by our interpreters! It was impossible, as far as I could see, to descend this so-called watercourse in any sort of vessel; but there was no point in protesting. I couldn't make myself understood to the Hounis and I was too exhausted to embark on a conversation in sign language. Furthermore, day was about to break and they were now clearly anxious to start back and get home to China. In the dark, I looked round for a secure hiding place for the daytime. I left the track and skirted a little paddy field on the bank of the stream. It was backed by a hill covered in fairly thick jungle. Here, I decided to lie low.

The porters unloaded my luggage on the rising ground not

far from the paddy field and gave me to understand that they were about to set off on the return march. As agreed, I scribbled a note for Long, telling him I had safely reached my goal. Not wishing to worry him pointlessly, I informed him that all was well, whereas I was firmly convinced of the contrary. The Houni gave me a deep bow, collected his men together and disappeared in the dark. I found myself alone in the silence of the Indo-Chinese forest.

This was the moment for which I had been waiting for weeks, the moment when, left to my own devices, I hoped to perform wonders. My first sensation was a feeling of unbounded freedom. How strangely satisfying it was to be cut off completely from the world. Good-bye to the exasperating ritual of Chinese courtesy, farewell to Colonel Song and his spitting, to hell with the careful collation of useless information from unreliable sources. Even at Pin-Ku-Yin, even in the hamlet of Ti-Nah, I was someone labelled and classified, no doubt with a very detailed file in various French, English and Chinese government departments. Here, I felt completely anonymous. No one in Indo-China suspected my presence.

My first task was to look for a more secure hiding place. It would soon be light and some peasants might possibly turn up in the paddy field. With a great effort, in several trips, I moved the whole of my equipment twenty yards deeper into the forest, scrambling up the slope of the hill. I kept slithering on the heavy soil, which the rain had made as smooth as ice, and this simple operation took me a good hour. At last I was installed with my baggage in some thick undergrowth which seemed to provide reasonable cover, albeit in an extremely uncomfortable position. Stretched out on a muddy slope at an angle of forty-five degrees, I was obliged to wedge my feet against a tree trunk to prevent myself from slipping. I was so tired, however, that I slept in this position until dawn.

Dawn, a grey dawn, found the former P. J. Rule, ex-rubber planter, ex-Burma Roader, ex-adviser to the government of Chiang Kai-shek, covered in an astonishingly thick coating of mud, soaking wet, devoured by leeches and ants, with bare bloodstained feet, lost somewhere up in the crags of Upper Indo-China, lying prostrate beside a curious assembly of bamboos and various other oddly shaped objects including a sort of half moon, a piece of inner tubing that had belonged to an American truck.

I was in a forest of wild banana trees, and the rain dripped slowly from the huge leaves. I recognised the smell of decay, characteristic of the jungle. I was awakened by the light, the rain and the pain I felt in my feet after last night's march. Congealed blood and mud formed a solid crust swarming with ants and leeches.

I took the risk of an unwelcome encounter and made my way down to the river to bathe in the clear water. Returning to my hiding place, I opened my inner tube and took out the cigarettes and matches I had stowed away there under cover. I was at last able to have a smoke and above all get rid of the leeches by burning them off, a process familiar to all bush-whackers. The knife, Fan's precious gift, helped me to clean up the lair where I would have to keep hidden all day. Then I unpacked my supplies, stodgy rice and grilled meat, and ate my first meal, washed down with the Thai alcohol which made me take a brighter view of my odyssey. On several occasions I heard voices: peasants walking along the path I had taken last night. But they moved off without suspecting my presence. Refusing to think of the following night and of how I was going to leave this hiding place, I spent the day in a curious state of dazed semi-consciousness.

Second night

However great the difficulties of navigating on the narrow stream on which I had been landed by the joint efforts of the Chinese, Thais and Hounis, I made up my mind to attempt a descent. I had no choice. With my baggage and raft, it was out of the question to set out on foot. By following the stream, maybe towing the equipment behind me, I hoped to reach a broader river, then the Nam-Na.

I set to work shortly before nightfall. I carried my equipment piece by piece down to the water's edge. I assembled the raft and lashed down my bundles. These operations took me over an hour. The Chinese rope, which was now damp, was extremely difficult to handle. I kept tearing the skin off my hands while tightening the knots. When the stowing was at last finished, night had fallen. I sat down in the midst of my baggage and pushed off into midstream. I did not get very far.

Swept away by the current, I was hurled against the banks at every bend: my raft turned broadside-on and got jammed every other second between the narrow banks. After a time I felt a blow on the forehead which stunned me. I had not noticed a plank that served as a bridge lying across the river. I found myself hanging by my neck, unsaddled, while my vessel continued on its way. Luckily it did not get very far and landed on some shingle. I caught up with it and mounted it again. But I was unable to handle the bamboo which served me as a paddle because of the narrowness of the channel. It, too, now got jammed between the two sides. I clung on to it and once again the vessel was carried off without me. In the dark, I skinned my knees on the pebbly bottom as I floundered about to retrieve it.

I realised I couldn't go on like this indefinitely. But it didn't last long. After a sudden bend I found myself in front of a sort of weir, below which there was no longer any watercourse. To be more precise, there was no longer *one* watercourse. It broke up into a series of little channels which probably served for irrigation. I found myself washed up against the dam. It could not have been a worse place to choose: I was now out of the forest, bang in the middle of the paddy fields. I could see the dark outline of a hut a few yards off, and a dog started barking.

I expected the owner to emerge at any moment and there

was nowhere for me to hide. With my feet in their present condition, I could not even take to flight. In any case, I was in a completely dazed state, not yet fully aware of the nature of the impasse in which I found myself. I remained sitting for some time on the pebbles, gaping stupidly at the little channels disappearing into the grass.

Something had to be done, however. I abandoned raft and bundles and started off at random in the dark, following one of those little streams which perhaps flowed into a larger river. I spent most of the night wandering about like this in the paddy fields, up to my knees in the mud, trying to find my way through the labyrinth of channels. It was a depressing reconnaissance. They kept intersecting, parting, twisting round on themselves, then petering out in a forest of tall grass. I was afraid of getting lost and so retraced my steps to try and get my bearings. One of those blasted channels led me up to the foot of the mountain, then back again through endless meanders to the point where I had left my equipment. I suffered agony from my legs, which were cut and bruised and once again covered with leeches. I was just beginning to think I would never extricate myself when, on one of my wanderings to and fro, I found myself facing a river, a real river almost like a torrent. It was not the Nam-Na, but possibly one of its tributaries. Allah be praised!

I toiled like a porter for the rest of that memorable night. I had to dismantle the raft and, in four trips, stagger through the mud carrying my vessel and baggage to the edge of the river. I knew I had to get clear of the house before daybreak, and the prospect of leaving this blasted valley gave me new strength.

All that remained was to re-assemble the equipment. My hands, softened by the water, found it more and more difficult to manipulate the searing rope, and further strips of skin were torn off. While I was fiddling with the knots, a light appeared a hundred yards away. I forced myself to go on with my stowing as calmly as though I were on a quiet beach.

More haste, less speed. I knew that if the two sections of bamboo were not firmly attached and the bundles lashed down so as to withstand the jolting, I was doomed to failure. So I carried on with my work and paid no attention to this light, which presently disappeared.

I was now ready for a second attempt. I boarded the vessel and pushed off.

It would be difficult, I'm afraid, for anyone to understand the sensations that assailed me straight away.

I was utterly exhausted. I subsided onto the raft as one sinks back into an armchair, desperately hoping to stay put in that position all the way to Hanoi. As soon as I was in midstream I felt as though I had plunged into a dark abyss and was incapable of making the slightest effort to master the invisible forces driving me along. I couldn't see a thing. In the mountains, in the paddy fields, I had grown accustomed to the *darkness of land*. The darkness of the river was no more intense but it was *different*. I was not used to it. I forced myself to think, but although I kept telling myself I was being swept along in a strong current and ought to take some action to control this impetus, how was I to convince myself of a fact so contrary to appearances? My eyes were unable to discern the banks, unable to discern the trees. The only sense which could have guided me was the sense of touch. But the water in which I was sitting, into which I dipped my hands, seemed as calm as the waters of a lake. Unconsciously I recalled the old theory of relativity; then, revolted at the idea of thinking of Einstein at a moment like this, I tried nevertheless to peer through the gloom above this black sheet heaving all round me.

Another burlesque, extravagant sensation, which made me fear for my reason: a dark mass, whose shape I was unable to discern, went gliding *past* my raft at what seemed to me a dizzy speed. I repeat: it went *past* me. I sat gaping, plunged all of a sudden in a wonderland. In a flash I pictured a crocodile, even a shark, one of Fan's giant tortoises, a tiger amusing itself by racing against me, an elephant. A few seconds later another dark mass caught up with me, grazed against me as it went past and disappeared in the darkness in *front* of me. I was far too flabbergasted even to feel frightened. This went beyond the wildest imagination. Prodigious things were no doubt happening on earth, for this time, my eyes, which were beginning to grow accustomed to the new conditions, had discerned in this dark mass a tree, a tree surrounded by bushes, a tree standing upright, racing along at the speed of a galloping horse. And it was followed by others, and then a pile of rocks. All these objects left me standing, appearing to jeer at my immobility. In my dismay, a funny Marseille story I had heard in my youth suddenly flashed across my mind— Olivier gets out of a car moving at fifty miles an hour, in the belief that it has come to a stop, because Marius has just passed him in his Alfa Romeo at a hundred and fifty. I found my adventure just as droll.

But it wasn't the spell of the wonderland. After a blaze of rambling conjectures, the truth dawned on me and the mystery vanished: *I was moving down-stream backwards.* In the gullet into which I had been inhaled when I pushed off into the current, an eddy, unbeknown to me, had no doubt spun my vessel round so that I was now being swept along back to front. It was the trees and rocks standing motionless on the bank that had given me the illusion of rushing past me. This departure from the usual position of the traveller, who sees the countryside coming to meet him, had sufficed to plunge me into an enchanted universe. Another of Einstein's little tricks.

I came down to earth. I now considered my position. With my anxiety increasing now that the spell was over, I began wondering how this was all going to end.

It ended rather badly. The djinn of the forest, who had protected me in the wonderland in which I had taken refuge, abandoned me as soon as the spell was lifted. I crashed into an obstacle at water level, was flung into the air, then swept

141

through some reefs in a flurry of gurgling spray. My raft was behaving like a drunkard, lurching from rock to rock. This was a real torrent, all right, but it wasn't very deep. My legs, which I had left dangling in the water, dragged against the bottom, scraping on every pebble, and I didn't even have the wits to lift them clear. I made no attempt to steer the vessel in this swirl and expected to see it smashed to bits at any moment. I had already heard some ominous cracks and each fresh jolt gave me a pang.

Yet my raft held out and my baggage did not fall off. In the midst of the tumult, I had a feeling of pride at having built this vessel with my own hands. As far as I could judge, this descent lasted about twenty minutes, during which I must have covered three or four miles.

After this I experienced another strange sensation: flat calm after the storm. As though at a stroke of a wizard's wand, the waters subsided, the rocks vanished, the banks melted away. I found myself in the middle of a vast tranquil lake. This, at least, was the impression I had, the first (rather quaint) idea that flashed through my mind: the torrent came out into a great lake that was not marked on any map. I felt as though I was once more under a spell. I had to adapt myself anew, to force myself once again to peer through the shifting gloom, to discern the trees moving on the distant banks, in order to realise and gradually acknowledge that the torrent had simply joined a deep broad river. It was the Nam-Na! It could only be the Nam-Na, and drifting on its waters seemed a restful pastime in comparison with the descent I had just made.

As the truth eventually dawned on me, I experienced a magnificent sensation of triumph. I had overcome all the snares of the mountains and the river. Nothing could prevent me now from reaching Hanoi. I felt almost drunk with delight as I recalled the hazards of the last two nights. I stretched out voluptuously on my raft, gazing up at the sky, in which a faint pallor announced the coming dawn.

Day was about to break. It was the hour when the beasts of

the jungle seek a secure hiding place; it was the moment I too had to go into hiding. I drew closer to the bank in search of a landing place. I was now able to estimate more accurately the speed of the current in relation to the land. It was still very swift. The tranquil lake I had imagined had disappeared. It was only at the influx, and in the absence of any point of comparison, that I could have thought I was on stagnant water.

In fact, the aspect of the river was changing every minute. The speed of the current was now increasing second by second. The flat mirror forming the liquid surface began to be swept by ripples, almost unnoticeable at first and at rare intervals. Then the intervals grew more frequent and the waves increased. At the same time the faint rumble which announced the approach of some rapids grew into a roar. The low-lying banks drew closer and became two walls of granite. The darkness grew more intense. I negotiated the rapids, once again the plaything of the waves and eddies, with a sensation of my own impotence. They were less violent, however, than the previous ones and I emerged safe and sound after a few minutes; but they had acted like a cold shower on my optimism. Hanoi was far away and I was not yet in the plain, where the rivers flowed unhindered through paddy fields.

Day was breaking. I had to stop. I sighted a narrow beach bordered by thick forest. I hauled my raft up onto the bank. Without having enough energy to dismantle it and put it under cover, I lay down in a bush and fell asleep at once.

I was awakened by a blistering pain. The sun was already high and blazing down on my sore legs and hands. Legions of ants scuttled over my limbs, but the leeches had mercifully disappeared.

As on the day before, I methodically set about putting myself to rights. I did what I could to clean the deep gashes caused by the rocks and the Chinese cord. I had no medical supplies, but I came across a tin of talcum powder among the food. (I never understood how it had got there!) I sprinkled it at random over my hands and feet, which soothed the blisters a little. I had something to eat and drink, then smoked a pipe, pondering on the next night. It was about ten o'clock in the morning.

Just then I noticed an angler on the opposite bank. The sight of this living creature horrified me. I thought I was ten leagues from the nearest inhabited spot. I lay flat on my stomach behind a bush, without daring to move. I had finished my pipe some time before and felt an irresistible urge to smoke another, but my tobacco lay with my bundles a few feet away and I would have had to come out of cover to retrieve it. I stayed where I was, contemplating this inoffensive-looking person through the branches. From that moment on I have never been able to see an angler without wanting to strangle him. This child of the Thai country had all the gestures, all the attitudes of his brethren on the banks of the Seine. He had the same patience and obstinacy, the same silly mania for struggling against an adverse fortune in a spot where he never caught anything. This went on for two interminable hours, after which he finally gave up and disappeared into the forest.

I inspected my raft thoroughly. It hadn't suffered unduly. I had to tighten the ropes, however, and fasten the bundles more securely: operations which caused me martyrdom. I had to use my teeth to tie the knots. Two bamboos had split and were letting in water, but this didn't detract too much from the overall buoyancy. Then I waited impatiently for the dark, vowing to keep going all night so as to make up for the time I had lost.

Third night

Another alarm, just as I was about to set off: three Thai peasants appeared on the opposite bank, squatted down at the water's edge and started talking in a conspiratorial manner. No doubt I was in the neighbourhood of a village. It was a stroke of luck that I happened to have chosen this bank on which to land. These three fellows once again imposed a severe strain on my nerves. Darkness fell over the river at last. They melted into the gloom of the forest and I decided to embark.

The first few moments of the descent were calm and everything pointed to a successful trip. Alas, this didn't last long. Who will one day sing the treachery of the torrents in Upper Tonkin?

I thought I knew all about rivers. I had negotiated them in rowboats, canoes and kayaks. I was familiar with the eddies of the Rhône, had known what it was to capsize in the icy waters of the Durance, and to hurtle over rapids with one of the crew crouching in the prow of the canoe and taking the full force of the waters on his chest so as to divert them from the vessel. I knew how to tackle abrupt bends—always on the outside of the curve, where the current was swifter but the water deeper and less full of snares. I had learned to distrust whirlpools which spin you round in a flash, cross-currents which jam you up against the bank, rocks just below the surface which tear the bottom out of a canoe and reveal themselves to a trained eye by a motionless wave in the midst of other waves in motion. I knew all this, yet I found myself as helpless in this dark as a townsman who had never travelled further than his office. I was unable to see the obstacles. Even if I had been able to see them, my raft was not sufficiently maneuverable to enable me to avoid them. I raced blindly round unexpected bends without knowing where the current was taking me. I was not aware of the presence of a whirlpool until I was caught up in the swirl and spun round like a top. Like a sightless man, I strained my ears for all I was worth. It was an unforgettable sensation to hear, above the continuous gurgle of the water, the roar, faint and distant at first, then rising to a deafening din, of some rapids approaching in the dark. I was soon subjected to the same impressions as on the previous night, only more intensely, for this time the obstacles were more dangerous.

The fun and games now began. The prelude was a distant

music, like the murmur of a crowd. The river began to dance and my raft followed suit. It was like a slow waltz. The dark surface heaved in a gentle swell. I was rocked to and fro as though in a hammock. Gradually the orchestra played louder and quickened the tempo until there was a continuous muffled roar, above which I could distinguish the clamour of several watercourses dashing through channels varying in width. At the same time the surface grew more choppy. The raft imperceptibly broke into a fox-trot as I was lashed by the flying spray.

Here I was, on the threshold of some frenzied bacchanal. The music had risen to an extra-human cacophony compounded of thunder claps, the pounding of a cavalry regiment, the shrieking of a hurricane and the cries of drowned men. The waters had now begun to jitterbug and I plunged into the typhoon.

I was stunned, bludgeoned by a fearful mass of water. I had only one thought in my head, only one desire: to remain clinging, clamped to my raft. All my remaining strength was mustered in the service of this one thought: not to let go of the raft. Then I was dragged down with it to the bottom of the river.

To the bottom of the river! It might seem unlikely that a structure of bamboo could be transformed into a submarine, contrary to all the principles of physics. To believe it, one would have to have witnessed the fury of the mountain waters when, in the bottom of a gorge, they meet a mass of rocks trying to obstruct their course towards the sea. It's a merciless struggle and all the more unforgettable when one takes part in it at night on a raft. The river's insidious weapon in this battle is to split itself up into an infinity of furious veins which escape in cataracts in all directions and reunite further down-stream in a seething mass.

I came to the surface again a few minutes later, still clutching my raft. I was safe and sound. It was a miracle that couldn't last. A dark shape suddenly loomed up ahead of me.

This time I actually saw the obstacle. It was a tall rock dividing the water into two parts. It loomed up out of the dark a few yards in front of me and the crash took place before I had time to move a muscle. It was less violent than I had feared. The cushion of water which had built up in front of the reef deadened the impact considerably. Only the tips of the bamboos touched the stone, but the raft reared up, bounced into the air, turned over like a pancake, and I was flung off, still grasping my useless paddle.

This was one of the strongest emotions I felt in the course of the trip; but the gods of the river had decided to subject me to an endless alternation of despair and hope. They had just stripped me of my indispensable equipment; they restored it to me immediately afterwards. As I was swimming, or rather struggling in the undertow, gulping a breath of air whenever I could, the shapeless familiar mass of my raft came bounding towards me like a faithful dog greeting its master after a long separation. I stretched flat out on the bamboos, managing with great difficulty to keep my balance, for the river was still jitterbugging. There was no end to these rapids. Furthermore, the raft had been overturned in this encounter. My bundles were now underneath. I prayed to heaven for the rope to hold.

And now, out of the gloom to which I was beginning to grow accustomed, there loomed up a sheer cliff which seemed to bar the torrent completely. How would the waters make their way past this obstacle which seemed impassable? Through what mysterious, maybe subterranean labyrinth did they pursue their course? It was a wall without any visible opening, so high that I was unable to see the summit, into which I was obviously going to crash. It would have been absurd to struggle, absurd to try to avoid the obstacle, for there it was, straight in front of me. I waited for the impact with resignation, without even attempting to use my paddle as a fender, intent on hanging on to the raft at all costs.

Yet the crash never occurred. Once again I experienced the strange phenomenon which I have already mentioned: the cushion which built up in front of any obstacle lashed by the current once again prevented a violent jolt. It was quite a curious experience to feel oneself being hurled towards the wall, to see the rock a foot away from one's nose, to brace oneself for the crash, then to be slowed down by a reactive force as powerful as the first, as though one were going up a steep slope after a descent. The raft, brought to a stop by invisible hands, was once again lifted up, tossed into the air, diverted from its original course, spun round and finally swept back in the opposite direction by a counter-current flowing along the foot of the cliffs on the left bank.

There, over a stretch of thirty feet or so, the waters were calmer. This was the first respite I had had since my departure and I tried to think rationally.

As far as I could see, as far as I could conjecture, the river seemed to describe an inverted S formed by two abrupt bends, the first to the right, the second to the left. What gave me the impression of a solid wall was merely the continuation of the cliff forming the left bank. The current came up against the rock and split into two separate veins. One of these flowed up the river; this was the one I was on at the moment. Conclusion: to extricate myself, I would have to get over on to the right bank.

Execution: I let myself be carried as far as possible on the counter-current; but it weakened and presently petered out. I found myself drifting back in the normal direction. At this stage, wielding my improvised paddle for all I was worth, cutting straight across the current, I tried to get as far as possible from this blasted left bank. Alas, I made little headway in this direction, my square-prowed vessel moving like a tortoise in spite of my efforts. Presently I saw the fatal wall loom up again. I weighed my chances with a certain amount of anxiety. Was I going to be flung to the left or to the right? In the former case, I would embark again on the original cycle. In the latter . . . the way to Hanoi lay open. The gods were unfavourable: it was to the left that I was flung, after yet another toss, towards that blasted left bank with the sheer cliff face. I repeated the same maneuver a third time, a fourth, a fifth, and it was always the same deadly cycle that started again, punctuated by a few seconds of fright each time, when I felt I was going to smash into the rock.

I finally realised I would never extricate myself in the dark. I would have to make my way much further up-stream if there was any chance of my getting to the right bank. I was unable to do so by water, for the counter-current did not carry me far enough, or by land, for the cliff rose sheer and there was no means of approach. I was at the end of my tether and decided to halt until daybreak.

Feeling my way in the dark, I tried in vain to find an accessible spot. The tips of my fingers encountered an absolutely smooth surface, without so much as a twig onto which I could cling. Incidentally, in the course of this feverish reconnaissance, I was caught up once again in the interplay of the currents and once again went through the infernal cycle, this time involuntarily. Was I going to keep turning in circles forever? This appeared to be the fate in store for me—for me and the bits of driftwood that kept me company on this endless roundabout.

Something would have to be done about it. As I was once again drifting past the cliff, I caught sight of a peg of land rising eight or ten feet above the water, a sort of truncated island with some uneven surfaces. I managed to hang on to it. Then, with a heave of which I shall be proud till my dying day, I hoisted myself up, together with my raft. How did I manage it? This is one of the few details of my odyssey that I no longer remember. I should have been incapable of it in cold blood. I only know that I didn't even bother to dismantle my vessel, which in any case would have been an impossible feat in the dark and in the water. I dragged the whole thing up in one fell swoop.

My final memory of this incident was, first of all, poising the fully laden and insecurely balanced raft on the tip of the truncated cone. Next, I managed, with a great effort, to open my parcel of food and get out the bottle of Chinese spirit which I drained to the last drop. After that, I lapsed into unconsciousness without daring to stretch out completely on the bamboos for fear of the structure toppling over.

I must have remained in this position for about two hours and woke up chilled to the bone, cramped and aching in every limb. It was still dark. It had started to rain. I was soaked to the skin, I hadn't a single piece of dry clothing to put on and my teeth began to chatter. The shower, coming on top of the cold dip, had revived a dormant germ of malaria. I had an attack of fever on top of my perch and my shudders kept shaking the raft in a most disturbing manner. Yet I was absolutely longing to sleep, otherwise I would be incapable tomorrow of facing further effort and strain. But how could I sleep in this icy rain which was tantamount to a Chinese torture? I had no covering except half a towel, which was wringing wet like everything else. I then had an idea which seemed nothing less than a brain wave: I curled up once more on my platform, squeezed the towel as dry as I could, then held it in both hands above my head. Improbable though it may seem, I fell asleep in this incongruous position. Every quarter of an hour or so the towel, which was once more soaking wet, would let the water through and I would be drenched. I got into the habit of wringing it out without waking up completely, then dozing off again. I spent the rest of the night like this and did not fully recover consciousness until sunrise.

It required all my will power to rouse myself from this position, which was dreadfully uncomfortable, yet in which I would have gladly remained for days and nights on end. For the first time, perhaps, I began to doubt my powers of endurance. The night before I had felt an absolute need to rest and had glimpsed the possibility of failure.

I forced myself to go through the routine of any civilised man on waking. I climbed down from my perch, washed my hands and face and brushed my teeth. Then I ate a further ration of rice mixed with sugar. Finally I looked round for some means of getting out of this cul-de-sac.

I had not been wrong in my conjecture. The rising sun revealed the S of the river, just as I had pictured it, albeit somewhat less regular. In fact, it was a good thing that I had not tried to escape from the circle the night before and been carried to the right. I would have been swept into a narrow channel between the cliff, which jutted out like a promontory into midstream, and a sort of needle which prolonged it. I would have inevitably come to grief in this channel bristling with rocks. There was no way through except by hugging the right bank and to do that I would first have to make my way still further up-stream. By day the maneuver was possible, perhaps. I decided to attempt it.

In cold blood, unfortunately, I was incapable of lifting my equipment all in one piece. It was now wedged between the rocks on top of the cone (there was no risk of its toppling over). With rage in my heart I resigned myself once more to carrying out the operation which cost me a greater and greater effort each time: unfastening the bundles and dismantling the two sections of bamboos. Then, panting for breath, alternately swimming or hauling myself up the cliff by my hands, occasionally even managing to find a foothold, I gradually moved the various pieces of equipment a reasonably safe distance away. All I had to do now was assemble the whole thing again in the water (this mission of mine really was an endless succession of fresh starts) and re-embark. I started off, cutting across the current perpendicularly, trying to reach the right bank above the dam.

Out of the corner of my eye I saw it hurtling towards me. I now realised the danger of being only partially successful, that is to say, of being sucked into the narrow channel in midstream. It would mean the end of my adventure. I paddled as hard as I could, aiming at a tree on the bank, without daring to glance at the dam on my left. This was the crucial moment.

151

I was exactly level with the needle. The raft, slowed down by the backwash, tilted once, twice; I closed my eyes. When I opened them again, I gave a shout of delight: the spirits of the river had sent my vessel down the auspicious side. I was swept along in a surge of spray towards the open river—toward Hanoi.

It had been a close thing. The reaction set in once again and I savoured the thrill of success. But all these maneuvers had taken me most of the day. It was three in the afternoon. The watercourse was now calm. I landed on a sandy beach and, starving from these emotions, gobbled up a huge quantity of rice and grilled meat. Then I held a sort of council of war with myself.

Though I had overcome a fair amount of difficulties, I had not made much headway. At this rate it would take me not six days, as I had expected, but a whole month to get to Hanoi. My original plan to move only at night seemed impractical. I was in the middle of the jungle, far from the nearest human being, or so it seemed. I decided to make part of the journey in the evening, before nightfall, and also in the morning, at first light, at least as long as I was in the hill country, where navigation was too hazardous by far and where inopportune encounters were unlikely.

I therefore set off again about five o'clock. The bumpy descent of the rapids began, but what a difference now that I was no longer blind! Daylight dispelled the phantoms and gave every obstacle its true shape. I was once again jolted, shaken, thrown against rocks and dragged to the bottom of the river, but I could fight back and managed to maneuver between the reefs. When the water was calm, as it sometimes is between two rapids, I indulged in the luxury of looking round me, admiring the extraordinary beauty of this waterfall and the gorges through which it flowed. I was even so entranced that I forgot my precarious position and the hostile night to come. I glided in silence between two chains of mountains already swept by shadow, along countless meanders, encountering

152

round each bend a valley wilder and more enchanting than the one before.

Presently all I could see was the sky and the ribbon of water threading its way between the dark masses of the cliffs. Then the nocturnal phantoms rose again all round me.

Fourth night

I tried all the same to pursue my voyage in the dark, but was soon at grips with the same perfidious obstacles as on the preceding nights. So I decided to stop until morning. I believed I knew exactly where I was, having checked my position with three successive tributaries. Tomorrow, at dawn, I would descend a further twenty miles or so. Then I would have to halt again this side of a village slightly north of Laichau. There I would hide during the day, for the subsequent stage could only be undertaken by night. I would have to go right past the village, then past Laichau, where I would at last meet the Black River. After that, it would be only one day more to Hanoi.

I stopped on a pebbly beach just before some rapids whose roar promised further hazards to come. After the thrill of the struggle against the elements, I was overcome for the first time by the sensation of loneliness, overawed at finding myself in the dark in the middle of the jungle that was now hostile. Every moment I fancied I heard the stealthy tread of a tiger. One of the Hounis had remarked in an off-hand manner that there were quite a lot of them in this region. Fan's knife would be a feeble weapon in the event of such an encounter. I hadn't had time to worry about this before. I had a revolver with me, granted, but was it still in working order after its long immersion in the water? I decided then and there to try it out. The noise of the shot reassured and comforted me a little. All the same, I left the raft at the water's edge, ready to re-embark at the slightest alarm.

I hadn't had a stitch of dry clothing on my back for four days. I wrung out my shirt and put it on again still damp. It began to rain, an icy rain, and I had another bout of fever. The only way I could keep more or less warm was to do half an hour's exercise on the beach, tired out though I was. Then, instinctively adopting the position of animals at rest in the jungle, I coiled up so as not to lose any body heat, snuggled under a bush and fell into a restless, feverish sleep.

I set off again at dawn and immediately afterwards found myself being tossed about in some more rapids. I knew I could only press on for an hour at the most, after which I would have to hide so as not to arrive in broad daylight near the village. The first part of the trip was uneventful, but just as I had decided to stop and look for a hiding place, the malign spirits of the river played me a final dirty trick.

In spite of my efforts, I was swept down an uninterrupted series of rapids. The Nam-Na, which up to now had been broad, had closed up so as to form no more than a narrow channel, where the water cascaded rather than flowed between steep banks. I tried in vain to land. Impossible to steer my raft in these foam-flecked waters which no longer had any consistency. They were nothing but eddies, whirlpools, geysers, which flung me from one bank to the other without my ever being able to catch hold of these inaccessible walls. Feeling extremely anxious, for I could not have been very far from the village, I dived overboard and tried to swim ashore, dragging my vessel after me with one hand. Total failure: the liquid vein held me fast and would not let me go. This lasted for two or three miles, I believe, which I covered at a dizzy speed.

Then the banks drew apart and grew lower all of a sudden. As though emerging from a tunnel, I came out in broad daylight on to a plain of paddy fields and saw some Thai peasants at work in their fields.

This was disastrous. They noticed me at once and showed their astonishment by shouting at me from the bank. By an ironical stroke of fate, the river was now quite calm and I could easily have landed. But where could I have hidden? I

decided to push on as quickly as possible. I waved my hand
in reply, blithely hoping to pass myself off as an inoffensive
tourist.

A pirogue put out from the bank and the boatman soon
caught up with me. We glided along side by side. He addressed
me in a language of which I didn't understand a word and
motioned me to follow him. I shrugged him off. Whereupon he
started paddling as fast as he could, shot past me and went
ahead.

I was more and more worried. Indubitably, the alarm
would be sounded throughout the region and I was bound to
be arrested at Laichau. I simply had to find some hiding place
until nightfall. Round a bend in the river I found myself in
another forested area. The place looked propitious. I waded
ashore, intending to drag my vessel into the undergrowth. As
I was feverishly dismantling my bundles and bamboos, the
bushes parted and two or three dozen Thais advanced towards
me.

3

LAICHAU

The villagers formed a semi-circle round me; it was impossible
to escape. I decided straight away to bluff it out and try to
pass myself off as an eccentric sporting tourist. At the head of
the Thais was an Annamite who spoke French reasonably well.
I greeted him with a composure that I was far from feeling
and told him the following story:

My name was Routin (I had to ransack my brains to fabricate this name). I was a planter from Cochin-China and
had spent the last few months with a colleague of mine, prospecting the jungle in Laos and Upper Tonkin. After a long
tour we had reached the Nam-Na Valley and, our work
being completed, I had had a bet with my friend that I would
reach Hanoi by the waterways.

The little Annamite listened to me in astonishment. Yet I
told my story with such composure that he appeared for a
moment to believe it. I played the simpleton and innocently
asked him what the name of this spot was. I pretended to be
delighted that I was only ten miles from Laichau and told him
I would press on as far as that town and then stop and rest for
a couple of days. He replied that this was out of the question,
because, so he maintained, there was a dam and a waterfall
up-stream from the village which no vessel could possibly
negotiate. I would do better, he added, to stop in the village
for the day. The mayor would put me up and send for some
horses so that I might get to Laichau overland. I realised at
once it was pointless for me to refuse this offer. I knew the
villagers had orders to arrest anyone they found entering the

territory without permission. I accepted his offer with a show of enthusiasm and, escorted by the whole group, made my way to the mayor's.

The *tri-phu*, or village headman, questioned me with a suspicious air. After telling him my story (the Annamite, who was his secretary, acting as interpreter) I adopted a haughty attitude and demanded a bed and a meal. I was told I would be given both.

Ostensibly, I was treated as a guest. But in fact I was kept under close watch by the partisans who had gathered outside the mayor's. I was obviously going to be taken to Laichau and handed over to Major F. I started thinking once more of this character who was said to be on our side and had agreed to a meeting with us, and my hopes revived. Yet, if he was to be able to do anything for me, assuming he was willing to do so, I would have to make sure of avoiding any fuss or publicity. I would have to continue to bluff it out, conceal my true identity, simulate a clear conscience and, if possible, make the story I had invented on the spur of the moment sound as plausible as possible. For the time being I could do nothing except eat, rest and sleep, for I was in rather poor shape.

I checked my bundles as they were carried in by the *tri-phu*'s servants and had them put in the room that had been set aside for me. My suitcase was there. I resigned myself to demolishing the little masterpiece of packing that I had accomplished with such effort, and cut open the waterproof sheeting. My clothes were intact, and so were my papers and money; not a drop of water had filtered in. I realised there was enough material here to lead to the arrest of at least half a dozen people in Indo-China and so decided, before doing anything else, to destroy certain letters. I could not light a fire and burn them for fear of alerting the guards who kept watch on me without appearing to do so through the window and the slit of the door which did not close properly. I therefore tore them into small pieces and mixed them with water so as to form an illegible porridge. As for the other documents, which compromised no one but myself, I kept them. I still entertained a wild hope in the success of my mission.

With my mind more at rest, I indulged in the rare luxury of having a shower, bathing my sores in clean water, drying myself with a towel, donning a clean shirt and trousers, socks and shoes, and shaving carefully. I did not recognise myself when I looked at my reflection in the mirror. Five days' departure from civilised habits had altered my appearance completely.

Afterwards I came out of my bedroom and sat down to the meal that had been prepared for me. In less than ten minutes I gobbled up a whole chicken, a huge omelette and a tureenful of rice. I derived a childish pleasure from eating food on a plate, using a fork and drinking out of a cup.

After the meal I had to linger a few moments and chat with the mayor's secretary who would not leave me alone. The story I had made up seemed to fascinate him and he kept asking for further details, which I invented and described with a self-assurance that surprised even myself. Then, insisting on the fact that I was very tired, I withdrew to my bedroom for a siesta. I was closely guarded: there were some partisans lolling against the wall beneath my window and two of the *tri-phu*'s servants shamming sleep just outside my door. All of a sudden I felt the accumulated fatigue of the voyage. I could hardly stand on my feet and the dysentery I had caught in China began to affect me again.

I lay down on the bunk which served as a bed and, after resting my head on my suitcase, which still contained some precious papers, lapsed into unconsciousness.

It was dark when I woke up. Still feeling somewhat fuddled, I heard two French voices whispering outside my room and a sound of horses informed me that the *tri-phu* had received reinforcements. I caught the words: 'Leave him until to-morrow. I'll post some guards over him.' After that I was once more bludgeoned by sleep and did not wake again till the morning. I got up, bright and fresh, and would have felt almost fit had it not been for the confounded dysentery. I dressed, sauntered out of my room and came face to face with an inspector of the Native Guards, Lieutenant Y.

Clinging with the force of desperation to the character I had created the day before, I launched into an act that was to test my nerves to the limit for a week. I greeted Inspector Y. with the enthusiasm of a traveller lost in the desert who at last encounters a fellow human. Without giving him time to ask a single question, I apologised for entering a military territory without a permit and remarked with a touch of irony that the worthy Thais who had put me up no doubt took me for a pirate or smuggler. I told him my story about prospecting from Cochin-China through Laos and Upper Tonkin and of the famous bet I had had with my colleague. It was by no means perfect, but I could think of nothing better. I was a prisoner of this fable, on which I elaborated to my utmost to make it plausible. I assumed the role of a sporting type, a bit of a daredevil and show-off, and my efforts to strike the right note imposed a severe mental strain. In a self-satisfied manner I asked him if he often came across chaps like myself wandering about on a raft in a region like this.

I fancied, for the time being, that the fish was biting. Maybe I had some hitherto unsuspected talent for acting; I would need it in order to make him swallow a yarn like this. Y. looked rattled, taken aback by my self-assurance. Our relationship, after ten minutes' conversation, was established on a basis of cordial egality, whereas he had probably arrived the day before with the intention of arresting me. I had reached the goal at which I was aiming: he did not even ask to see my papers. He was not to ask me for them for a week. I felt I had summed him up accurately. He was one of those nice, rather weak chaps who hate offending anyone.

I did my best to avoid any dangerous questions and went out of my way to switch the conversation from myself. I apologised again for entering Laichau territory without a permit. In an artless manner I asked Y. if I could go into town and report to the local commander. He was delighted. For the last few minutes I had noticed how diffident and undecided he was, not knowing how to set about asking me to accompany him to Laichau. He declared it would be a pleasure for him to come with me. However, he added, I would not be able to see the commander for several days *since he was on tour near the Chinese frontier.*

Imagine with what interest I pricked up my ears on hearing this news! Had F. finally gone to the meeting he had promised Long? My hopes soared: I managed to convince myself that this was what had happened. If he had seen Long, it meant he was definitely on our side and that my problem would be solved. All the more reason for continuing to play my part in front of Y. and the French at Laichau, which would make his task easier if he were willing to save me. I therefore replied that I would be delighted to spend a few days at Laichau while waiting for the commander's return. The inspector was more and more pleased: I was anticipating his every desire. The conversation grew friendly and he confessed with a laugh that he had come to Laichau with the firm intention of arresting me. We both thought this an excellent joke.

We set off on horseback with an escort of native guards. I did my utmost to keep up a conversation and chattered away, sensing that in the intervals of silence Y. was pondering on my extraordinary odyssey and was bound to find it rather improbable. I spoke about Cochin-China and Annam and, thinking it would be clever to mingle fact with fiction, casually mentioned that I had been mobilised in Phu-Bai Camp. Y. then told me that the assistant administrator of Laichau, M.Z., had likewise been called up at Hué in 1940. Fresh cause for worry. I vaguely remembered Z., who was then an officer cadet. We had never been in the same unit but no doubt we had acquaintances in common. This was not going to make my explanations any easier. What on earth had possessed me to talk about Annam?

We eventually reached Laichau after a two hours' ride along a fairly decent track. Here I was introduced to Z., civilian assistant to Major F. I remembered his face from the Hué days all right, but he did not recognise me. I had changed since then. I had lost over fifteen pounds, my features were drawn and I had grown a moustache. I played the same game as with Y. I said I was going to wait in Laichau for the major's return, adding that I would be very glad to see him because we had several friends in common (another invention). All the same, I was not so naïve as to think this story would be swallowed wholesale; but, so long as there was some doubt about me, they would not, perhaps, in the absence of their superior, take the responsibility of arresting me. It seemed to succeed.

I left my luggage in the little hotel in Laichau, where I was given the best room. Y. asked me to have lunch with him. I dared not refuse and yet I badly wanted to be alone. There were just the two of us and I was on tenterhooks. I could no longer prevent the conversation from coming round to my trip and at every second I was in danger of being shown up as an imposter. Little by little the story I had invented developed and assumed proper substance, while I made a mental note of all the details I was obliged to fabricate as I went along, so as to avoid contradicting myself later. This, therefore, was the odyssey of P. Routin, the former P. J. Rule, in which truth was cunningly mingled with falsehood, and which took shape as a result of random question-and-answer in front of a spell-bound inspector of the Native Guards.

Routin worked in Cochin-China for a plantation company which up to then had dealt exclusively in rubber but was thinking of extending its activities: hence the object of my mission in Laos and Upper Tonkin. For the time being, this consisted simply of prospecting the forest with a view to establishing a future network of plantations in the mountains. Plantations of what? I hastened to forestall the question I anticipated on Y.'s lips. I was not allowed to give details, which for the time being had to be considered as 'confidential' (this again struck me as being an admirable invention). I hinted, however, that it concerned a very extensive and as yet secret plan for the economic organisation of the country, supported, but behind the scenes, by the Government . . . Whew!

These 'confidential' matters and 'the clandestine support of the Government' seemed to leave the worthy Y. aghast. I came back to them each time I was asked an embarrassing question, assuming a more and more security-conscious manner, until the inspector finally gave up interrogating me on this point.

As for the itinerary I had followed, I quickly realised that the inspector, who had been in this part of the country only a short time, was not at all familiar with the region I claimed to have travelled across. So I embarked on an orgy of specific information, juicy details of this months-long trek through the jungle that my imaginary colleague and I had made together. We had crossed reputedly impassable mountains, hunted elephants, tigers and panthers. We had lost most of our equipment in a torrent and, to round off this tall story, I asserted that my colleague had made his way back with our escort, resolutely recrossing the mountains just to have another look at a certain district that had struck him as being particularly interesting, whereas I, who had always had a passion for boating, had decided to get to Hanoi by an original route.

I ended up by insisting once again on the confidential aspect. We had not been reported by any military post in the region? The explanation was simple: our mission being top secret, we had always avoided all inhabited places. I insinuated that I would be able to account for myself more thoroughly to the local commander when he got back.

While pouring out this stream of absurdities with the greatest composure, I anxiously studied the expressions on my host's face. Astonishment, doubt, incredulity, then a certain admiration and finally, I fancied, conviction could be read in succession on his features. Granted, it was unlikely that I should have embarked on this expedition without official permission and I trembled at every moment, expecting him to bring up this point. But he still did not ask to see my papers. I believe he didn't dare to.

After the meal he saw me back to the hotel and left me there, on my own and ostensibly free. His departure delivered me from an unbearable tension. After locking the door of my bedroom, my first reaction was to fling myself on the bed and give vent to an outburst of wild laughter.

And indeed, drama and farce were so closely mingled in this adventure that I no longer knew how to react. I was utterly bewildered. Should I take advantage of this apparent lack of surveillance and try to escape? Give up my attempt and try to get back to China through the forest? With the alarm sounded and in my present physical condition, I would have little chance of succeeeding. Should I on the contrary go on bluffing it out and place my fate in the hands of F.? I weighed the pros and the cons for the rest of the day and most of the night. Eventually I made up my mind: I would stay and wait. Damnable decision. It was either blindness or weakness that prompted it. No doubt, without admitting it to myself, I was frightened of facing the jungle again.

I got up late next morning. The hotel boy came up and told me there was a gentleman downstairs who wanted to speak to M. Routin. I wondered apprehensively what this new character was after.

I found myself in the presence of an old colonial, tanned and desiccated by the tropical sun. He was a planter from the neighbourhood of Laichau. He had heard that a planter from Cochin-China was passing through and had very kindly come to welcome him to the North. He was getting married next day to a local Thai girl and wanted to ask me to the wedding breakfast. The whole European colony of Laichau would be there, he told me, and everyone who had heard about me and my exploits would be delighted to meet me. I was far less enthusiastic about this myself and would rather have been sealed up in a tomb than face further questions. But the old boy would not countenance any excuse and I was obliged to accept his invitation.

Shortly afterwards I had a call from Z., the assistant administrator, the man who had been mobilised in Hué. He had come, in fact, to have a chat with me about Hué and Annam. I thought it advisable to give a few precise details and recall some actual memories of Phu-Bai, which would at least prove that there was some truth in my story. I managed to refuse his invitation to dinner, on the grounds that I was extremely tired, and spent the rest of the day in my room reading some old newspapers.

Next day I was introduced to the entire French colony of Laichau at the wedding breakfast. In addition to the bridegroom, the bride (a ravishing Thai girl), Y. and Z., all the garrison officers were there: a captain, two or three subalterns and a young cadet* who were familiar with the region, having done several tours of duty here. It was going to be a hard job to maintain my superb self-assurance. The captain launched the first assault.

He congratulated me on my sporting exploit and asked me if I had called at a certain post where one of his friends was stationed. This post, he told me, was situated right on the route I had taken and I could not have missed it. I replied that I had indeed called there but that the commanding officer had been absent so that I hadn't stopped. This bewildered the worthy captain, who could obviously not believe that his friend had deserted his post. He darted me a glance full of suspicion. A bad start. I was on tenterhooks. I managed to switch the conversation to another subject, but a certain uneasiness persisted.

Luckily, there is any amount to drink in a garrison in Upper

---

* This cadet was, like me, a native of Avignon and a member of a distinguished family. I recognised him at once by his name, his resemblance to his brothers whom I had known, and the inevitable jokes about Southerners which the other officers made. It's a small world out East!

Tonkin on the occasion of a wedding breakfast. I must have drunk about as much as all the rest put together. The captain, who had also had a skinful, returned to the attack. He could not understand why, after travelling over such a long and arduous route, my colleague had gone back the same way instead of making for the nearest centre of civilisation. 'He has a passion for mountains,' I said. 'What about you?' the mulish fellow retorted, gazing at me with his blue eyes. 'Me? Oh, I have a passion for rivers,' I replied in a peremptory tone and with a touch of impatience, for this idiot's obstinacy was beginning to irritate me.

I managed to slip away at the end of the meal, not without being subjected to the assaults of the bride and bridegroom, who insisted I should come that evening to the Thai feast which was being given in their honour. But I had had enough; I excused myself on the grounds of another bout of dysentery and rushed off to take refuge in the solitude of my hotel.

And this went on for seven days! Seven days, during which I played the part of the hare-brained Routin, seven days during which I felt suspicion growing, during which Y. hovered round me with this simple question on his lips: 'Have you any papers?'—a question which I always managed to nip in the bud by humbugging or assuming a distant and mysterious manner. At one moment I would ask myself if I had done the right thing in deciding to confide in F., and the moment after I would be full of blind confidence in my impending interview with him. Improbable though it may sound, it was only after six days of hesitation, on the eve of his return, that I regretfully decided to destroy some detailed documents bearing on the sabotage of certain bridges useful to the Japanese.

Y. eventually turned up one day in my hotel bedroom, from which I now hardly ever emerged, and told me the major was arriving that night. I said I was glad to hear it and applied for an interview next day.

The next day was a Sunday. At eight o'clock in the morning Y. introduced me to Major F., with whom I immediately requested an interview in private. He had been told my story and was peering at me with curiosity. He ushered me into his office and closed the door behind him. I told him:

'My name isn't Routin; I didn't come from Cochin-China and I'm not prospecting. I'm an officer, I joined Free France in 1941 and I'm now engaged on a mission in Indo-China. I've come from China, where one of my colleagues sent you a message asking you to meet him. We were told you had agreed to this in principle. Unfortunate circumstances have landed me in Laichau while I was trying to get to Hanoi. I want you to help me.'

The major listened without interrupting and replied in measured tones: 'I am and always shall be loyal to the Marshal, who knows what he's doing. I consider the Free French are mistaken and are acting against the interests of our country. It is therefore impossible for me to help you.'

So that was that. I tried to plead my cause, which I did rather clumsily, however, having no gift of persuasion. He listened to me politely, but it soon became obvious that any discussion was pointless.* Having refused to help me, all that remained for him was to arrest me.

He did so, abiding by the usual conventions. First of all he asked me to have a drink, gave me half a dozen packets of cigarettes, which I was weak enough to accept, then dismissed me . . . and had me escorted by the wretched Y., who accompanied me back to the hotel, informed me with a blush that I was under arrest and tactfully began to search my luggage. It was plain that he had never undertaken such a task before.

I left the hotel and was led into a room in the barracks, equipped with strong bars. But the outward forms of courtesy were still respected; a bed and a table were brought for me

---

* I never felt any sterile resentment against him. It was my own fault and not his that I had gone so far as to imagine he had the same ardour and enthusiasm as ourselves. Yet I have since heard that he has never forgiven me!

from the hotel and I was able to have meals sent in from outside. I was at the end of my tether and incapable of the slightest reaction. I was not to understand fully what was happening to me until my arrival at Hanoi.

I was transferred there two days later, by car, accompanied by Inspector Y. and the administrator Z., both of them stiff and ill at ease, and an armed Annamite rifleman who seemed deeply intrigued by his prisoner. The journey, by way of Laichau, Sonla and Hoa-Binh, was uneventful except for the night we spent in Sonla.

We arrived there in the evening, myself in rather poor shape as I could not get rid of my dysentery. Outside the Residence a jailor spitefully brandished a huge bunch of keys in my face. He had no doubt been told that an unexpected client was to spend the night there and was clearly delighted with this windfall which broke the monotony. An inspector of the Native Guards stood beside him and I recognised him as one of my former colleagues from Phu-Bai Camp.* He also recognised me and shook me by the hand. Then he went off with Z. to discuss my case with the Resident of Sonla, who eventually turned up and ushered me into his office.

The Resident looked extremely perturbed and did not quite know how to express his sympathy. He told me I would be treated as a guest during my sojourn in his domain and simply asked me for my word of honour not to attempt escape until the next morning. Physically incapable of attempting escape, I gave him my word.

Thereupon I was introduced to several other Frenchmen stationed in Sonla and invited to a big dinner by my friend from Phu-Bai Camp, which I could have well done without, but I almost had the impression of being the hero of the day. After the meal I was buttonholed by a young subaltern from the garrison who likewise insisted on declaring his complete sympathy towards Free France.

I was beginning to feel embarrassed and also, I must admit,

exasperated by all this display of friendship. I was expecting either outright hostility or else a sense of comradeship manifested in deeds, not words. But what could I think of fellows who seemed to be saying: 'Well done! Good show! You're a splendid fellow. We feel the same as you do. But, mind you, we're going to haul you off to prison.' Admittedly, none of them could have done anything for me at the stage I had now reached.

I left Sonla in the morning after spending the night in a comfortable room. We reached Hoa-Binh at dusk after being ferried several times across the Black River, which I had hoped to reach on my raft. We were out of the mountains and on a fairly decent road. We had been descending continuously all the way from Laichau and were now crossing the last hills, beyond which lay the valley of the Red River.

Y. stood me a farewell meal at Hoa-Binh. Next day I was to be handed over to the authorities in Hanoi. I kept the conversation off this subject. We left early next morning and one of my last sights of the free world was a vast plain covered in paddy fields: the delta of the Red River. I had come full circle. Here I was, back in Indo-China, which I had left in high hope about a year before. After making a long detour through several countries in Asia, I was almost back where I had started from, flanked by two guards.

We drove into Hanoi and drew up outside the military prison. Y. and Z. looked more and more uncomfortable. I now made acquaintance with those characters who shamble through life with a bunch of keys in their hands and strict instructions in their heads. The one who received me confiscated my watch, my matches, my knife, my shoe-laces and then searched me. I said good-bye to Y. and Z. and was led into a tiny dark cell where I was left alone with my thoughts. The great adventure was over; it had ended badly, in utter defeat. The one that now began was less exciting, and also less amusing.

Prisons
1942–1944

The memoirs of a prisoner can scarcely be set down as a continuous narrative corresponding to the dreary procession of each hour, each day or even each month. To follow this procedure would amount to imposing on the reader a boredom as unbearable as that suffered by the captive himself. I shall record only a few incidents which stood out as slightly less dismal landmarks in the course of the monotonous march of time.

COURT MARTIAL

October, 1942

'Prisoner at the bar, stand up . . .'

Before the colonel had stopped speaking, the hefty gendarme behind me gave me a thump in the back with his elbow and hissed in my ear: 'That means you. Stand up.'

My behaviour in court seemed to be a matter of grave concern to the hefty gendarme who had come to fetch me that morning from the military prison of Hanoi, accompanied by a colleague. He was used to this sort of ceremony. He had spent a long time inspecting my turn-out, insisting, with his profound knowledge of humanity, on the fact that military magistrates are always susceptible to well-polished shoes and a clean collar. He had harped on the same string all the way to the courtroom:

'Speak up . . . Look straight in front of you . . . Above all, don't forget to stand up each time you're spoken to.'

He wanted his prisoner to be a credit to him. Right from the start I had been conscious of him standing there behind me, restless, anxious, on tenterhooks, watching my every gesture, forever hissing in my ear: 'Now then, watch out.' His manner was beginning to annoy me even more than the farce I was witnessing.

'Prisoner at the bar, stand up . . .'

In the shuttered silence, the unsteady voice quavered and died away. Unlike the hefty gendarme, the colonel presiding over the court was not used to this sort of ceremony. He looked awkward and ill at ease, like a novice.

And indeed he was a novice, as anyone could see. Assigned by fate to this fatigue duty, he had already made two mistakes in the prescribed ritual, which he must have boned up on yesterday from some manual. Major P., the government commissioner, who exuded professional self-assurance from every pore, had corrected him with a formality verging on sarcasm. Now there was the ghost of a smile on the major's lips, for the voice had trilled 'Stand up' in a shrill falsetto. I stood up all the same.

'Your surname and Christian names?'

This time the words resounded like a thunderclap. Humiliated and furious at his lack of self-assurance, the colonel had bellowed. All the members of the court (a major, two captains and a short-sighted subaltern, as far as I can remember) jerked upright in their seats and my advocate (a little Annamite who had been assigned to me according to regulations) was so startled that he dropped his briefcase. It was now his turn to look ill at ease, all eyes being turned on him while he picked up his scattered papers. My hefty gendarme cast a withering glance in his direction. At the end of the room a squad of a dozen soldiers under the command of a warrant officer waited in silence to present arms at the end of the hearing. I did my best to be as patient as they were. Meanwhile the colonel had recovered a little composure.

'Your surname and Christian names?'

'Boulle . . .'

Another clap of thunder, even louder than the first. This time it was I who had bellowed. Was it bravado, or something to do with the acoustics? Or did I too lack experience like a novice? The hefty gendarme was desperate and cleared his throat to warn me of my incorrect behaviour. Major P. himself had given a start. The short-sighted subaltern frowned sternly. The colonel looked absolutely flabbergasted.

'Age?'

'Twenty-eight.'

This wouldn't do at all. We were now both out of control, oscillating between deep theatrical tones and high-pitched warbles punctuated by senile splutters. It took us several sentences to achieve an approximately normal manner of speech. The interrogation continued by fits and starts. The hefty gendarme was almost panting for breath.

'What have you got to say in your defense?'

'Here we go,' I sadly reflected as I saw Major P. spring up in his seat like a jack-in-the-box and start to wave his hands violently. 'Here we go, he's bungled things again.'

He had indeed bungled things! His papers were in a muddle and he was immersed in the notes he had carefully taken yesterday. 'The witnesses, the witnesses,' whispered Major P. The colonel flushed and looked daggers at him, but had to yield to his experience and therefore grumpily summoned the witnesses.

There were two of them. The first was an old acquaintance: the inspector of the Native Guards who had arrested me at Laichau, Lieutenant Y. I had summed him up accurately: he was without malice. He gave his evidence, then went out of his way to depict me as the most well-mannered and good-natured fellow in the world, unaware that he was annoying not only the judges and Major P. but also me, who could willingly have dispensed with this good-conduct certificate. The hefty gendarme was the only one to appreciate his statement and nodded his approval.

'He was very decent about it,' Lieutenant Y. kept repeating, 'he was really very decent indeed.'

The government commissioner eventually put an end to this evidence, which was utterly irrelevant, then glanced enquiringly at the colonel. The colonel flushed again, looked nonplussed and fumbled with his papers. Major P. thereupon decided to speak in his stead and asked me if I agreed on the facts. Yes, I agreed on the facts. 'Well done,' the hefty gendarme whispered in my ear.

A fresh silence ensued, followed by another perfidious

glance of inquiry at the colonel from the major and the sound of rustling paper. The major, like a good fellow, again prompted him under his breath: 'Any questions? Any questions to put to the witness?'

'Have you any questions to put to the witness?' the colonel grumpily repeated.

My little Annamite advocate now saw fit to intervene and asked a question which had no bearing on the matter in hand. The inspector spluttered and resumed his litany:

'He was very decent about it, very decent indeed . . .'

Eventually Major P. took it upon himself to make the court proceed to other matters. Exit the inspector of the Native Guards. Enter the second witness. This was the police commissioner who had conducted my initial interrogation. I can still see his flabby opium-addict's figure.

The commissioner swore to tell the truth, the whole truth and nothing but the truth, as the colonel complacently asked him to do.

He wasn't a bad fellow, the police commissioner. He was only doing his duty as a commissioner, as Major P. was doing his duty as a public prosecutor, and the hefty gendarme his duty as a hefty gendarme. It was not his fault that he and some of his colleagues had had to interrogate me in relays for about fifteen days and fifteen nights, allowing me all the same an hour or two's respite from time to time. On these occasions he would tell me he hated carrying out these duties, which may have been true. He sometimes had some sandwiches and iced beer brought in and would consume the lot in front of me. He did not behave like this out of nastiness, but only to obey orders. Higher authority had given him instructions to use every means to obtain the list of my accomplices in Indo-China. The commissioner had not used *every* means. He had not even resorted to third degree methods; he had not laid a finger on me. He had merely deprived me of sleep, food and drink and relentlessly fired questions at me, always the same questions. It was not even he, I remember clearly, it was not even he but his colleagues who relieved him, who threatened me with the execution squad, who declared they would be forced to hand me over to the Japanese, while reprisals would be carried out on my mother in France. He merely indulged in vague allusions. He was a bit of a bumpkin, in fact.

But this wasn't at all serious, it was just a lot of eyewash. When he had carried out his orders for fifteen days and fifteen nights and thus fulfilled his mission, he had a large meal brought in for me. And then he had looked surprised and genuinely grieved when I asked him if he was *also* going to allow me to drink: genuinely, truly grieved and shocked.

In the courtroom he seemed on the point of falling asleep. Major P. stopped him as soon as he began to speak and, with a great gesture of condescension, declared that the prosecution waived the evidence of this witness since the prisoner acknowledged the facts: enlisting in a foreign army and entering Indo-China clandestinely. He turned to me:

'You do acknowledge these facts, don't you?'

As I was opening my mouth to correct the term 'foreign army', I was winded by a jab in the stomach from the hefty gendarme, who chose this method of reminding me that I had to stand up whenever I was spoken to. I turned on him furiously, but he gave me such a touchingly responsive look that my anger evaporated at once. Resignedly, I rose to my feet and acknowledged that I had enlisted in the Free French forces. The colonel, who had lost control of the proceedings, tried to retrieve himself and interjected:

'Do you regret it?'

This was his bad day. The great moment had not yet arrived. Major P. had to correct him once again. The colonel bridled and could be heard muttering under his breath. It was bad policy on his part to have shown his feelings; from then on the major no longer gave him a helping hand. The silence persisted, until it became almost unbearable. It was the clerk of the court who volunteered to save the situation. 'Witnesses for the defense,' he prompted in a stage whisper. I could hear him from where I was standing.

'Call the witnesses for the defense,' bellowed the colonel.

It really was his unlucky day: there were no witnesses for the defense. I took pity on him and muttered to my little advocate: 'Tell him there aren't any.' The latter told him, after pulling at his cuffs as great lawyers do, and in his strange accent which was full of false stresses:

'M'lud, we have no witnesses for the defense.'

By now the colonel was sweating blood but made an heroic effort to save face. He leaned towards one of the members of the court and whispered in his ear, as he had seen magistrates do in the films, hoping, against all evidence, that the proceedings would follow their own course without any further action on his part. But Major P. was merciless and persistently mumbled: 'Ahem! ahem!' Crimson with shame, the colonel was forced to ask him what he ought to do next. The major smiled and said out loud: 'Ask the prisoner if he has anything else to say.'

The colonel asked me if I had anything else to say. I had originally prepared a lengthy speech, then had gradually whittled it down to a single sentence which I have since forgotten. I believe I said that I refused to recognise the authority of this court in any way. But I spoke in a tone of such bland politeness that all the members seemed quite pleased. They were obviously expecting a torrent of abuse. There was a collective sigh of relief and Major P. was so delighted that he stopped being unco-operative and spontaneously whispered: 'Regrets . . . regrets . . .'

This was the big moment. The colonel took his cue at once and peremptorily asked me if I regretted my behaviour. Everyone leaned forward and waited eagerly for my reply.

'No, Colonel, I have no regrets.'

My 'colonel' was instinctive. I had always been impressed by senior officers' badges of rank. Once again the polite trappings outweighed the content. The court seemed to breathe more and more freely. 'Right,' said the colonel contentedly.

Then Major P. took over officially and read out the charge, in which my crime was called treason and for which the prescribed penalty was capital punishment. Having read this out, he enlarged upon it.

He proved mathematically that I was fully responsible for my actions and pointed out that I had expressed no regret. The hefty gendarme shook his head as though in protest. The colonel raised his, relieved at having no responsibility to take for the next ten minutes or so.

The major proceeded to sum up. Having clearly demonstrated that in my case there were no extenuating circumstances, and proved that capital punishment was therefore the only just and logical penalty, he declared with complete inconsequence, and without giving any reason, that he would not demand it all the same. Hard labour was what he suggested.

He sat down again. I believe my little advocate then took the floor, but his speech had no bearing on the subject and no one listened to him.

The court adjourned to deliberate. The hefty gendarme led me into the waiting room and lavished words of encouragement on me, followed by further instructions. I must not, above all, forget to stand at attention while the sentence was being read out, and all would be well. My little advocate came in and shook hands. Not wishing to offend him, I thanked him warmly.

I was ushered once more into the courtroom. None of the members were there except for Major P., who was to read out the verdict. The sergeant-major in command of the squad gave the word of command: 'Attention.' I automatically snapped into that position. The hefty gendarme clicked his heels. The major began reading:

'In the name of the Head of State ... declares Lieutenant

Boulle guilty of treason . . . reduced to the ranks . . . deprived of French nationality . . . hard labour for life.'

Then he turned on his heels and marched out.

'Stand easy,' said the hefty gendarme, 'it's all over. It wasn't so bad now, was it?'

FRIENDS (AND CERTAIN OTHERS)

Some odd mental quirk has always prompted me to seek excuses for my enemies (and often to find excuses for them, as this narrative must have shown), which is no doubt the sign of an atrocious weakness of character. I remained true to this instinct during my spell of two years and four months in the prisons of Indo-China. I was never able to feel real animosity towards the humble warders who were merely doing their duty, even though their stupidity and sluggishness sometimes impelled them to acts of cruelty. But, even with the passage of time, I have not been able to extend this mansuetude to 'certain others', whose personalities are here roughly portrayed through their actions. I have done my best, moreover, to condense this remnant of as yet unneutralised ill-feeling into a single chapter, the present one, so as to have done with the unpleasant subject once and for all.

ROBERT'S EXPLOIT

January, 1943

On January 12, at seven-thirty in the morning, the inmates of Cell One heard that an unusual incident had taken place in the central prison of Hanoi. The demeanour and behaviour of the warder who opened the door that morning left no room for doubt on this score. The inmates of Cell One at this time were Labussière, Richard and myself.

But first let me introduce one of my greatest friends,

William Labussière, an outstanding fighter pilot with a brilliant record, one of nature's warriors, always rushing in baldheaded to support a righteous cause at the first sign of hostilities anywhere in the world; Labussière, who had taken part in the Spanish War, fought in China with the famous American 'Flying Tigers', whose commanding officer General Chennault, then a colonel, put on a par with the most eminent pilots among his compatriots—no mean praise coming from an American officer; Labussière, who had been pining away in prison for a year and a half already, for having tried to join Free France, taking with him the plans of certain Japanese installations in Indo-China; Labussière, whom the colonel presiding over the court martial had abused and grossly insulted during the trial, being likewise unable all the same to do otherwise after reading his record of service during the initial incidents with the Japanese, and being unable to prevent himself from angrily noting in the margin of the sentence he gave him: 'For his outstanding services in the Indo-Chinese Air Force, deserves to be pardoned, but only at the end of the present war'; Labussière, who had already at this period chalked up quite a number of days in the punishment cells for attempts at escape or lack of discipline and who was to raise this prize-list to an unbeaten record before the end of his captivity.

Richard had likewise been sentenced for similar reasons. As for myself, I had been in Cell One for about three weeks, after spending a month in solitary confinement.

As soon as our door was opened, then, we knew something unusual had happened. The warder shoved back Richard, who had approached to inhale the air in the courtyard, swore at the Annamite orderly, who was taking too long for his liking to put the tea urn down on the table, and fiercely declared:

'No exercise period today.'

The three of us looked at each other with surprise. Not that we expected any better treatment, but for some time (to be precise, since the American landing in North Africa in November, 1942) certain improvements had been noticeable in the hitherto harsh penitentiary routine inflicted on traitors of our sort: it had been decided, for instance, to move them from the dangerous criminals' wing and assemble them all together in two less inhuman cells, Numbers One and Two. At the same time I had been extracted from the dungeon in which I was in solitary confinement and lodged with my friends in Number One. As for Dr Béchamp, whom I shall refer to later, it had at last been realised that he was seriously ill and a decision had been taken to send him to hospital. All this had happened after the American landing in November.

'No exercise period today,' the warder yelled.

And he gave the orderly an angry kick in the backside, slammed the door behind him and bolted it noisily. But before taking to his heels, the little Annamite had had time to whisper a few words to Labussière as he put the tea urn down on the table.

'Robert's done a bunk.'

Right enough, there was no exercise period for us that day. We spent the rest of the morning praying for the success of the operation under way, while Labussière climbed up onto a rickety structure composed of a table and some benches placed against the door and tried to discern the manifestations of alarm which Robert's exploit had provoked among the prison staff.

One simply doesn't escape from a central prison! Robert had felt this adage did not ring true and had decided to prove its fallibility to our jailors. He had prepared his escape with the patience and pertinacity of the Breton that he was. He carried it out with the audacity of an ex-guerilla leader and the mastery of a professional housebreaker. This is the moment for me to say a few words about Robert.

Eugène Robert, a civil servant before the war and the father of two children aged one and two and a half, had taken part in the 1940 campaign, been mentioned three times in dispatches, awarded the Légion d'Honneur, and seriously wounded in a particularly hazardous raid, but had decided after the armistice that this was not enough and had sailed for Indo-China, hoping to find an opportunity to serve Free France. He had served for over a year, ostensibly as an Intelligence Officer in Tonkin, but in actual fact he was engaged in passing information to the Allies on Japanese troop movements. After the more or less complete occupation of Indo-China, he decided that his role in this country was not justified and, like Labussière, tried to cross over into China to join the F.F.I. Likewise arrested, with incriminating documents on him, he was sentenced to fourteen years' hard labour, with all the adjuncts that this distinction entailed at the time (loss of civil rights, disqualification from the Légion d'Honneur and, in his particular case, a few additional bonuses for him and his children, such as forfeiture of family allowances and confiscation of his assets in France). Robert, whom I had not yet met, occupied one of the two cells in which, after the American landing, the authorities had consented to assemble the 'Gaullist' prisoners.

So Robert, unconvinced of the aphorism 'One doesn't escape from a central prison', had gone out this morning on exercise with the firm intention of proving it wrong. It was no hit-or-miss attempt. For some time he had observed two facts that were worthy of interest: firstly, that his exercise period now took place very early, for the convenience of the warders, so that it was still quite dark in the tiny courtyard where he was brought to take the air; secondly, that a drainpipe, hanging half way down the wall, might enable him to reach the first outer wall if he managed to hoist himself up; thirdly, that in this courtyard there were some rickety old benches from which a sort of ladder could be improvised, by which means a monkey might stand some chance of shinning up the drainpipe and thus reaching the top of the aforesaid wall.

This was the chance Robert took, after spending several weeks secretly practising pull-ups. Reaching the top of the wall, which was capped with broken glass, he managed to make his way along it with the help of a blanket which he spread out in front of him, and ended up, of all places, in the head warder's quarters, the only part of the prison where there was no second outer wall, the other side of the building giving directly on to the street. All that remained was for him to tear through the dwelling like a whirlwind, no doubt sowing panic among the modest household, leap through a window on the far side, grab hold of the flagpole which decorated the building, drop ten or twelve feet to the ground, and land as though like a bolt from the blue at the feet of a warder and a sentry who were far too startled to react and had not even enough gumption to rush after him, since the rascal did not tarry there to explain the situation.

By now it was seven-fifteen. The sun had risen. Not being able to go at once to the safe house where he was hoping to find refuge, Robert hid in Hanoi Cathedral. He spent the morning in a confessional, then the afternoon in the belfry, while the enraged and frightened authorities decreed a practical state of siege in the town: patrols in the streets, road blocks with machine guns, vehicles stopped and searched, description and photographs of Robert in all the papers and a reward of five hundred piastres for any information concerning him.

After dark Robert crept out of his hiding place. He was lucky enough to be able to reach the house where he expected to find help. He found it after lengthy negotiations with several sympathisers, some of whom, however, were none too keen to involve themselves. But a reliable friend undertook to smuggle him out of the town the following night. Things were beginning to look up for Robert. He merely had to remain concealed in this house for another twenty-four hours, taking special care not to attract the attention of the Annamite houseboys who, as everyone in Indo-China knew, were particularly tempted by the offer of a reward of five hundred piastres. But on this point Robert's instinct failed him. He was wrong to fear any trouble from them. The Annamite houseboys didn't breathe a word.

It was a colonel who betrayed him;* a colonel who gave him away; a colonel to whom an agent had carelessly revealed the hiding place; a French colonel who had not merely refused his help but had picked up the telephone to denounce him to Headquarters, to General Headquarters at Hanoi, who in their turn immediately informed the Sûreté. (As I said, this was at the beginning of 1943, and, after their initial successes, the Allied armies seemed to be marking time in Africa.) I never discovered if the colonel cashed in on the reward of five hundred piastres. The philosopher I have since become still hopes to be enlightened on this point one day.

In Cell One, on this first morning, we were still in a state of euphoria and hope (mingled with regret at not having likewise taken advantage of the opportunity). Labussière's eye, glued to the spy hole, had a limited field of view, but what he occasionally glimpsed was enough to show what an uproar had been caused in the prison: warders running hither and thither and swearing at the Annamite orderlies, the arrival of several people in mufti accompanied by the head warder, policemen and officials from Government House. The obvious commotion and fury seemed to point to the fact of the escape having succeeded. If Robert were not recaptured during the next few hours, there was a chance he never would be. A visit from the head warder in the beginning of the afternoon reassured us on this point.

'Fancy Robert doing this to me, a man with a wife and two children!'

This was a personal complaint which had so little bearing on our present concerns that Labussière started quivering with rage.

'After all, haven't I always treated you as well as I could?'

This was fairly true. The head warder was not a bad fellow, unlike many others. He merely obeyed orders. And when (after the landing in North Africa) these orders had appeared

* It was from about this time that the impression made on me by senior officers progressively decreased.

slightly less strict, he had no doubt even done his best to grant us as many privileges as possible. We had a table and two or three chairs in Cell One, and even an armchair, which was brought in when Dr Béchamp was here (the doctor could not sit on an upright chair) and had been overlooked after his departure for hospital.

'This'll break me, or anyway lose me promotion. If they don't recapture him . . .'

'So he hasn't been recaptured!'

This was all we wanted to know. We felt almost inclined to embrace him.

'Meanwhile, you'll be the first to feel the effects. I'll have to move all this stuff out. It's not my fault; those are orders.'

'All this stuff' was the armchair, the upright chairs and part of our personal property which little by little (since the landing in North Africa) we had been able to recover. Two warders cleared the cell, while some others embarked on a thorough search.

'And that's not all,' the head warder went on, lowering his voice, 'we're going to have to make this up again.'

At these words we began to feel rather shaken, for 'this' was the fourth bunk in Cell One, the one which used to serve Dr Béchamp as a bed, the sheets of which had been folded up since his departure for hospital.

'We're going to have to make up this bed again,' the head warder repeated with a trace of embarrassment. 'The doctor's coming back.'

'The doctor . . .'

'This very afternoon. He'll be here soon. The M.O. rang us up . . . He's better, it seems . . . and besides, the M.O. has also been given strict orders to send him back here, at once . . . orders from the highest authority. You see . . . after all this fuss about Robert's escape . . .'

DR BÉCHAMP

An hour after the head warder's visit, and several hours after Robert's escape, the door of Cell One was thrown wide open to allow a strange procession to pass through. I saw a tall emaciated body, which looked as though it had been broken in two, flanked by two warders carrying rather than supporting it, for the doctor had practically lost the use of his legs and his lifeless feet dragged on the ground. But in his pallid, distorted face his eyes had retained an exceptional vivacity and no sooner had he been laid down on the bed than he gave us a wink accompanied by a smile, as though to say: 'I've heard about Robert. Good show!'

It was true; the warder had not lied. In Hanoi at this time there was a Medical Officer who was prepared to yield without a murmur to an administrative order and banish from his hospital someone as seriously ill as Dr Béchamp, who was prepared to send him back to a prison cell where he knew he could not be properly treated, just because another Gaullist prisoner had caused the authorities a lot of trouble. This M.O. was a mere colonel, no doubt; but the M.O. of a hospital, even if he is a mere colonel, has a hundred times more authority than a general. An M.O. is a sort of king, absolute master of his own domain. This one, however, yielded without a murmur to an order emanating from the Residency, which in its turn depended on Government House. He did not feel the slightest temptation to exploit his dictatorial authority but silenced his professional conscience as well as the sense of solidarity which it would have been natural for him to feel for a colleague, even if this colleague had been a criminal, even if this colleague had been an ordinary person, which was not by any means Dr Béchamp's case. He banished from his hospital a patient who was to die less than a month later for want of proper treatment. It is time, I think, to introduce the reader to the great Dr Béchamp.

No, the doctor was by no means an ordinary person. The

grandson of Antoine Béchamp, the famous nineteenth-century chemist, Dr Georges Béchamp had moved to China after the First World War. He ran a hospital at Cheng-Tu, while also serving as Consul of France. These activities absorbed only a small part of the doctor's intellectual activity, which was immense. After travelling all over the world for a number of years (what country had he not visited? what language did he not speak?) he had found in China a suitable setting for gratifying his passions: work, disinterested study, meditation and research.

I don't think there existed a single branch of human knowledge in which he had not at one time been interested, that he had not explored, applying to it a mind that was patient and methodical, granted, but also extraordinarily penetrating and thirsting for new discoveries. He was not a scientist in the usual sense of the word (he had an unconventional character which prompted him to diverge from the beaten track and he had a poor opinion of established schools) but in an extremely wide range of subjects he had acquired the competence of a specialist without losing his autodidactic originality. He had a profound knowledge of physics and mathematics and had even written a treatise on these subjects which he intended to publish at the end of the war. Though he had left Europe a long time ago, he still kept in touch with a number of scholars in the West (Professor Langevin in particular, I believe), exchanging a regular correspondence with them, keeping abreast of the latest scientific developments, incessantly comparing the tendencies and methods of various countries (the human aspect of problems fascinated him as much as the problems themselves), which had resulted in his complete mastery of English, German, Russian and many other languages.

I heard recently that he knew Father Teilhard de Chardin and that the latter never failed to call on him when his travels took him to the neighbourhood of Cheng-Tu. This didn't surprise me and I can well imagine what the conversation must have been like between these two minds, both obsessed with truth, both devoted to the pursuit of universal laws, starting from a patient study of experimental phenomena, both equally original, both also no doubt voluntary exiles, having failed to find in France sufficient encouragement and understanding among the coteries and cliques whom their audacious intellects disconcerted. It gave me the deepest satisfaction to know that Father Teilhard and Dr Béchamp were on such good terms, despite the poor opinion the latter had for most ministers of the Catholic Church—a fact which must be mentioned, for I feel it would be betraying the memory of this many-faceted character to conceal this side of his nature and in particular the poor opinion he had of missionaries. In fact he abominated them, lumping them all in a sort of world-wide conspiracy of hypocrisy (the only human quality, I think, for which he was capable of feeling hatred), and he held them responsible for all the evils from which China was suffering. But the doctor, who was no doubt an atheist, could expound on religious matters when he felt like it, as on anything else concerning mankind; even to the point of embarking in prison on endless theological discussions with the chaplain who, from time to time, got permission to visit us: even so much that his favourite reading was the Bible, the Bible in Hebrew, which the chaplain had brought him (though he modestly confessed that he was sometimes obliged to refer to the text on the opposite page, which of course was the Greek translation). No, Dr Béchamp could not have failed to be captivated by Father Teilhard's theories, and the latter was probably in a better position than anyone to appreciate the doctor's prodigious learning, his mind constantly intent on shedding all convention and his particular, not to say somewhat unorthodox, manner of confronting any problem.

I would have produced a very incomplete portrait of Dr Béchamp by depicting him entrenched in abstract theories and pure science. Technicalities interested him as much as science; art as much as technicalities. At Cheng-Tu he had a private workshop where he indulged in various experiments:

experiments which ranged from tests of radio apparatus to practical comparisons of methods of cutting metal with various implements on different Russian or American machines. When I saw him for the first time, he talked about rubber plantations in a way that showed there was nothing he didn't know about rubber trees. He could discuss music and painting with any art critic, and political economy with the most knowledgeable expert. As for his knowledge of French and foreign literature, I doubt if there was anyone who could compete with him in this field.

Exceptional erudition and a mind naturally sharpened and tempered by all sorts of intellectual speculation, always on the look-out for new ideas in every field, no matter how humble or trivial—these were not the least qualities of this remarkable figure. Dr Béchamp belonged to the little group of humans blessed by the gods, whom I have already mentioned, who show not the slightest hesitation at a crucial moment, who take the right decision in a flash and who never afterwards diverge from the line they have chosen, whatever might be the ordeals resulting from this choice. As early as June, 1940, the doctor had answered the Appeal, transforming overnight his consulate at Cheng-Tu into the Consulate of Free France, committing himself immediately and whole-heartedly to the cause he considered just, devoting to it his knowledge of the world, especially China and the Chinese, and helping, more often than not out of his own pocket, several volunteers to get to England.

Dr Béchamp was at Hong Kong in February, 1941, at the time of the capitulation of the town. Strange to say, it seems he was not bothered then by the Japanese. This is a mystery, for his name and his attitude were well known in China, but the solution is perhaps extremely simple and would be enough to restore one's faith in mankind. It seems not impossible for me (though it cannot be proved and may be nothing more than a novelist's fantasy) that the Japanese, a nation in which only the military behave like ruffians, an Oriental n tion, moreover, and, like the Chinese, with an instinctive respect for culture and wisdom, may have deliberately turned a blind eye on the actions of an elderly enemy (the doctor looked older than he was) because they recognised in him something rare and precious. This, I repeat, is only a personal hypothesis which no doubt betrays an absurd optimism with regard to mankind. It is equally possible that the Japanese failed to identify him. What followed, however, is certain. The doctor managed to embark quite openly on a Japanese liner taking some Frenchmen to Indo-China. He intended, when the ship called at Chu-Wan, to avail himself of this opportunity to cross the French zone, thanks to some Chinese contacts there, and return to Chungking. But though he had managed to escape the Japanese, he was not so fortunate with the French authorities in Indo-China. A launch laden with military police and gendarmes came alongside as the ship put in and the doctor was placed under arrest. He was subjected to the usual routine: fifteen years' hard labour, loss of civil rights, confiscation of his present property and any future assets, and solitary confinement in Hanoi Central—a sentence that was all the more harsh in this case, since the doctor, who was fifty-five years old but worn out by work and an arduous life, was in poor health and needed regular medical attention.

Dr Béchamp's condition had inevitably deteriorated since his arrest. I had spent about two weeks with him in Cell One before his departure. He used to spend most of the time lying on his bunk, and had to lean on one of us or clutch the back of a chair whenever he wanted to go and sit in the armchair. He ate nothing but a little rice, his stomach rejecting the somewhat unsavoury prison fare, and suffered two heart attacks, one after the other, which had at least contributed to his being sent to hospital.

When we saw him come back after being banished by the M.O., we were horrified by his appearance. We had to undress him and put him to bed. His condition was so pitiful that the head warder, after a moment's hesitation, decided to transgress one of the orders he had received and allowed the big pillow to be brought back, without which the doctor, who was afflicted by a deformation of the spinal column, suffered agonies.

In the evening Dr Béchamp, for whom the move had been a severe strain, recovered a little strength. We told him all we knew about Robert; he told us about his spell in hospital and confirmed the vileness of his colleague, the M.O. In spite of his physical condition he had lost none of his mental alertness and mustered enough energy to crack a joke or two. Then, while we lay down on our bunks, he immersed himself as usual in the Bible, either in Greek or Hebrew, the only book he had been allowed to keep. The doctor hardly ever slept. He merely dozed off for a few moments from time to time, during the day as well as at night.

We did not yet know that we were shortly to be separated, and this is one of the last recollections I have of him. I had the bunk opposite his. I woke up late at night and watched him without his knowing it. His book lay open in front of him, but he wasn't reading. Nor was he sleeping. His head was half muffled in the pillow, his eyes were wide open and his face looked even paler in the electric light which we had to keep on all night. No one was moving in Cell One; he believed we were all asleep. He seemed to be meditating profoundly. Suddenly I saw him stiffen, his features tensed, and I heard him murmur under his breath: 'What wretches those people are.'

We left him a little later and were never to see him again. Dr Béchamp grew weaker and weaker every day. His stomach reached the point of refusing all nourishment. He would stay in bed all day and had more and more frequent heart attacks. The orders of the Residency and Government House were nevertheless obeyed. It was not decided to send him to hospital until three months afterwards, after a serious stroke—three months, in other words, after Montgomery's victories in Tripoli and the retreat of the Axis forces in Africa.

In July he was transferred to Saigon Hospital, but lodged

in the cells of this establishment. It was not until November, 1943, after lengthy discussions with the penitentiary administration and the medical authorities, that he was admitted among the ordinary third-class patients and decently treated—in November, 1943; in other words, shortly after the Allied landing in Italy and the liberation of part of the peninsula. It was too late. Dr Béchamp died on July 20, 1944.

This was shortly after the landing in France, which for him was a special occasion. He was allowed to receive all the visits he wanted and a cascade of presents that were no longer of any use to him. Yet on the evening of his death, Robert, who was also in Saigon Hospital at the time, asked for permission to salute his mortal remains and was refused. His request was not granted for several weeks—not until the complete collapse of the Axis forces and the disappearance of the last doubts and last hopes cherished by the erstwhile supreme authorities in French Indo-China concerning a German victory.*

THE 'JUSTICE BAR' OF INDO-CHINA

This was the treatment inflicted on Robert as a penalty for flouting the authorities. But this punishment was not decreed by the prison administration; the order came from higher authority, the Residency and Government House—sixty days' solitary confinement, including fifteen with his feet in the 'justice bar'.

I was well acquainted with this medieval-looking instru-

* A letter I received a short time ago (1965) made me think once again of Dr Béchamp. What my unknown correspondent told me about him shows how interested she is in his case and what admiration she feels for his memory. It was she who informed me that he was a friend of Father Teilhard's and she wanted to know what posthumous honours had been bestowed on him, which clearly shows that a character like the doctor is not easily forgotten. I should explain that my correspondent is an American lady, Mrs C. S. Leiper. She lives in California; she is in no way related to the doctor, but even today she is continuing her research on him, simply because his case fascinates her.

ment, which at one time used to be much in evidence in the
Navy, a fact which may possibly explain why it was introduced at this period into the prisons of Indo-China. I was well
acquainted with it, for I had lived in its company in the cell
in which I had been placed in solitary confinement after my
sentence. The treatment was never applied to me (it had never
before been applied to any Frenchman but was reserved for
recalcitrant Annamites under sentence of death. Robert in-
augurated the new policy of a new order.) But I had had
ample leisure to examine it and ponder on its use.

The justice bar, the 'bar of Indo-China', consisted of two
parts: a fixed section, embedded in the cement, with two semi-
cylindrical cavities carved out of it, rather like the humps of a
camel in reverse. A second half, likewise of heavy cast iron,
pivoted on a hinge round the fixed section and was equipped
with two similar cavities which, when the contraption was
clamped down, fitted exactly over the first two so as to form
two perfect cylinders equal in diameter to that of the ankles of
an average man. For this, as the reader may already have
guessed, was the use to which this instrument was put: the
prisoner had his ankles inserted in it so that, once the bar was
locked and bolted down, he found himself flat on his back on
the concrete floor with his head turned to the ceiling and his
bare feet extending beyond the bar, unable to turn on to his
side and forced to indulge in extraordinary acrobatics in order
to use the latrine pail placed beside him by a benevolent
administration. The rules prescribed no more than five
minutes' freedom a day.

This was the punishment inflicted on Robert and it was in
this contraption that I saw him for the first time when Labussière and I were moved from Cell One and taken to the famous
building known as the Death Block, in which I had already
spent a month in solitary confinement and with which Labussière was likewise familiar as a result of non-compliance with
prison regulations. The Death Block consisted of several
individual cells giving on to a corridor. Each of these cells

measured seven feet by seven feet, and most of this space was occupied by a cement platform which served as a bunk, with its odd-looking adjunct: the justice bar.

One must be fair. We were entitled to a straw paillasse on top of the cement. Not Robert, of course, who was being punished and whose war wound, in the position which he was forced to assume, caused him agony. We were also entitled to spend twenty minutes every morning outside our cells in order to wash and stretch our legs in the corridor. Robert was entitled only to five minutes, but we would see him through the spy hole as we strolled past his door. Occasionally, after the initial burst of ill-temper caused by his escapade, some of the more humane warders even allowed us to exchange a few words with him in spite of orders. One of them even opened his cell for us one day and allowed us to go in and shake hands with him. We availed ourselves of this opportunity to tease him about his present position and tickle his shackled feet until he tried to fling his latrine bucket in our faces—for, make no mistake about it, our morale was as high as ever in those trying times.

I spoke just now of humane warders. Again one must be fair!—there were a few of them, at least at certain times. I think it was the head warder himself who had this ingenious idea to alleviate Robert's punishment to a certain degree. The orders were to place him in the bar, but they did not specify if the prisoner was to be fastened by one foot or by both. After lengthy cogitation he had the brain-wave of inserting one foot only, which enabled Robert, who was fine-boned, to swivel his ankle round in the hole and, by means of acrobatic contortions, occasionally to lie on his side or even flat on his stomach on the cement floor, a position which afforded him another view besides the ceiling. Compassion was carried even to the lengths of changing from one foot to the other every twenty-four hours!

Yet again one must be fair. The three of us, Robert, Labussière and myself, were not the only ones to be interned in the

Death Block. Not at all. Higher authority had decided that we should share these quarters with three real traitors who had *likewise* been condemned for treason: for treason, *like us*. They had sold some documents to the Japanese before the official period of collaboration. Great care was taken to treat us *all* in exactly the same way and, so as to make quite clear that there was not the slightest difference between their case and our own, a placard was erected for two days at the entrance to the corridor bearing the legend CONDEMNED FOR TREASON in big eye-catching letters—that is, until Labussière, having torn it down twice and threatened to put an end to anyone who replaced it, the head warder decided, for the sake of peace, to place it outside the building. He was an acquiescent character, as I said before, and always prepared to come to terms compatible with the orders he received in order to avoid a fuss.

We remained in the Death Block until June, 1943, at which time Government House decided to move us further back from the Chinese frontier and transfer us to Saigon (this measure had already been taken in Robert's case a month or two earlier). We travelled like convicts in a chain gang, the authorities taking great care to manacle each of us to one of the three real traitors I have mentioned, who nevertheless did not give us away when they saw that Labussière and I had succeeded in sawing through our handcuffs. Unfortunately there was no favourable opportunity for us to jump out of the train. The gendarmes of the escort caught on to our little game, but no disciplinary action was taken against us.

It was a different matter three months later, when Labussière made his memorable bid on his way to court, where he had been summoned for further questioning. This time he was handcuffed to Robert, who had grown so thin since the treatment inflicted on him at Hanoi that he easily managed to slip his hand out of the manacles. Robert made a break for it first, but was in such a weak condition that he was immediately recaptured by the gendarme escorting them. Labussière seized this opportunity and dashed off through the streets of Saigon with the handcuffs dangling from his wrist. The gendarme blew his whistle frantically, while Robert caught hold of him and held him back so as to give the fugitive more time. A regular man-hunt ensued. Labussière was eventually recaptured after an epic pursuit, with the handcuffs still dangling from his wrist, after beating up an inspector of the Sûreté and a passer-by who had rushed after him in pursuit. The penalty imposed on him was sixty days' solitary confinement. This time Robert escaped being punished, which appeared so unusual and suspicious to the Governor of Cochin-China himself, and no doubt so offensive to his keen sense of justice, that he went to the trouble of writing to the governor of the prison and demanding the reason for this compassion. But this time there was an M.O. who came forward and declared that Robert's state of health precluded his being placed in solitary confinement.

As for Labussière, since there was no 'justice bar' at Saigon, this instrument was replaced by some iron rings fastened round his ankles, which allowed him to move his feet. But, in order to make up for this relative comfort, he was left in these shackles for sixty days, in the more or less total darkness of a cell measuring six feet by four. Here he spent a Merry Christmas.

One must be fair, one must always be fair: our situation improved considerably at the beginning of 1944. Since the probability of a landing in France was now a practical certainty, even to the dullest mentality, the Governor of Saigon Central (a sinister imbecile, but who trembled more and more every day at the idea of what might happen to him later if we accused him of having maltreated us) decided to remove us from the dangerous criminals' wing, in which we had been kept for several months in the company of bandits and murderers, and transfer us to a separate building where we enjoyed relative comfort. This comfort progressively increased as the Allied successes continued, so that from June onwards, after the landing (which the governor made a point of announcing to us himself, as though this event were bound to forge some sentimental link between us), we were literally deluged with gifts which our friends delivered to the prison and which the administration now hastened to hand over to us, certain warders even supplementing them of their own accord with some little treat or other.

A strange period! Boxes of cigars and bottles of wine and brandy, sometimes delivered by colonels, littered the prison lodge. An odd period! The governor, who had put Labussière in irons, used to come in every morning to bring us the latest bulletins of the Allied broadcasting stations, unbeknown to his subordinates. Then these subordinates would come along shortly afterwards and bring us the same news, unbeknown to the governor. A touching period, when this very governor seriously studied the possibility of introducing some prostitutes into the prison for us to while away the time; when Labussière was able to tear down a portrait of the old marshal which hung in the infirmary and be met with nothing but sidelong smiles, as though everyone appreciated the joke.

From then on we were no longer isolated and began to have regular contact with the outside world by means of more or less clandestine messages and by visits lasting longer than the regulation time. At this juncture we heard that a great deal of interest was being taken in our fate by a number of people in Indo-China, such as Barrion and his friends, who had never forgotten us, others whose clandestine activity had prevented them from openly declaring their allegiance, and still others who had gradually manifested their sympathy for us since the beginning of 1944 and whom the prospect of a future Allied victory rendered all the more impatient, all the more eager to demonstrate by some spectacular act their attachment to the cause of Free France. It was then they began to talk quite seriously about engineering our escape.

3

AN ESCAPE

October-November, 1944
When the two gendarmes, accompanied by Inspector Bréart
of the Sûreté, came to Saigon Central Prison one evening to
take Robert, Labussière and me to the station prior to our
being transferred to another prison in Laos, there was no need
to see the conspiratorial winks they gave us to realise that some
important operation was being mounted, that if the gods were
favourable we would never arrive at this new jail, and that
this journey was to culminate for us in freedom. Though we
were unaware of the details, the *modus operandi* of the plot,
we knew the essential fact: we were going to be abducted in
the course of the journey.

Bréart was 'in the know'. He had been on our side for
some time. He was to accompany us in the train as far as Hué
to make sure everything had been properly organised, for our
abduction was to be engineered somewhere beyond that town.
The two gendarmes were in the know; they had decided to
come with us, which was bound to facilitate our escape. The
headquarter's staff were in the know; they had resigned themselves to helping us, since another project had come to their
ears which had seemed somewhat too risky (a project worked
out between us and Barrion, an old friend of ours, which consisted of hijacking the Air-France plane on its flight between Saigon and Hanoi, which Labussière would have then
piloted to China). There were several others 'in the know', as
we subsequently realised. In theory the operation should not
be too difficult during this transfer of ours to Laos, which had

been decreed by Government House. In fact, it was a happy coincidence.

Thus the escort came to fetch us at Saigon Central and, to hoodwink the governor who, unlike them, was not in the know but who probably suspected something was up, the gendarmes handcuffed us with a whispered apology. (They even feigned a superhuman effort to tighten our manacles so that the veins on our wrists stood out.)

The procession moved off. Lined up by the gates of the prison, the governor, the head warder and a couple of underlings waited for us to pass by, like family retainers. For two pins the governor would have shaken hands with us. But, confronted with our somewhat forbidding manner, he thought better of it. He gave orders for the heavy gates to be opened and, as we marched through, this puppet gave a bow and murmured: 'Good luck, gentlemen!'

There was a gendarmerie captain waiting for us on the station platform. He saluted us and asserted with a conspiratorial wink: 'I've given you some *good* gendarmes, *the best of the lot*.'* This sounded promising. We climbed into a coach and the train steamed out. Bréart, who had gone to get the latest information, told us that *it* would happen after Hué, during one of the numerous changes necessitated by the cutting of the line where the bridges had been destroyed by the American Air Force. There was therefore nothing to be done this first night but get some sleep, which was not so easy, considering the state of our nerves.

We reached Hué next morning. The programme entailed a day's wait in the town, since the trains only moved at night for fear of the air raids. The gendarmes wondered whether they should not handcuff us again for the sake of appearances. They decided not to when they saw our lack of enthusiasm.

---

* They proved to be good, not only on this occasion but also later on. One of them, Massac, was massacred, alas, by the Japanese when they took control on March 9. The other, Moustier, then joined a guerrilla group which operated for several months.

And so, walking freely for the first time in two years, we emerged from the station into brilliant sunshine. It was a strange sensation for me to find myself again in this town where I used to spend every evening when I was stationed at Phu-Bai Camp.

Our procession headed for the Sûreté. Bréart warned us to be prudent and above all to keep up the act. He was not quite sure which characters were in the know. But the demeanour of the Head of the Sûreté, who was waiting for us in person, reassured us. He gave us a conspiratorial wink fraught with understanding. He drove us off in his own car, first to the Resident, who apparently wanted to see us. The Resident in his turn gave us a conspiratorial wink which surpassed all the rest in mysterious significance. He had organised a little party in our honour to which two or three officials were invited. After that we were taken to the Hotel M., which I knew well, where a sort of semi-official banquet had been prepared for us. Everyone kept staring at everyone else, wondering in whom and how far it was possible to confide.

Then we were taken up to our rooms where we slept for a few hours under the guard of an inspector, while the conspirators went off into town to receive the instructions of their respective groups. The gendarmes came back in the evening, somewhat disconcerted by the situation which was getting out of hand. There were, as I have said, any amount of people in the know—the Gendarmerie, the Cochin-China Sûreté, the Civil Service, the Deuxième Bureau of the Army, the Annam Sûreté, the Native Guards. But the very person who had been chosen to escort us beyond Hué was a police officer who came from Tonkin, and he was not party to the conspiracy. (They must have searched high and low to find someone who wasn't, but there it was.) Bréart warned us about this before going back to Saigon, for his job was now over.

The gendarmes informed us of the outcome of the day's confabulations: the abduction would take place that night, during the first change of trains. A car would be following the train and would take us off to Hanoi. Some friends would identify themselves to us in the coach, who were ready to help us if necessary. Many of the railway staff were likewise accomplices.

'Tough guys, all of them, and ready for anything,' the gendarmes assured us, repeating what they had been told. 'There'll be nothing for you to do.'

'Real daredevils, never fear,' the Resident's assistant confirmed, as he brought us the encouragement and wishes of his immediate superior.

And there would also be, apparently, an emissary from the Deuxième Bureau in mufti to see that everything went off all right.

Fine! But there was one thing we would have to do, one of the gendarmes explained, brandishing a little phial he had been given. We would have to knock out the inspector who was to accompany us by giving him the contents of the phial to drink.

'What?'

'You see,' he went on, lowering his eyes, 'neither my colleague nor I could very well do it.'

This was true. They were already being extremely helpful. We could not reasonably expect a couple of gendarmes to do us the additional favour of slipping a Mickey Finn to a Sûreté inspector! Very well, then. We took charge of the flask, while Labussière, who had somehow got hold of a rubber cosh and hidden it under his shirt, grumbled that there were simpler ways of knocking a man out. Nevertheless we put our heads together and worked out a scheme, while the gendarmes made a thermosful of coffee to serve as a pretext for doping the poor wretch who was not in the know.

It was only too clear that he was not in the know. He was a rather dapper little fellow who must have received the most detailed orders and any amount of additional instructions from his immediate superior, the senior superintendent. He had come from Hanoi that morning, all cock-a-hoop over the confidential mission with which he had been entrusted. He had had surprise after surprise since assuming his duties and finding us cozily installed in the best rooms in the Hotel M., surrounded by boxes of cigars and quaffing a bottle of champagne, a gift from the Resident. He had opened his mouth to protest when he saw us strolling freely up and down the platform while waiting for the train, and again when he noticed one of the gendarmes slip us a hundred-piastre note, a gift from a friend, to buy some cigarettes and drinks.

He had opened his mouth but he had closed it again, in the throes of an incipient complex which made him feel as though he was the only member of his species. He now confined himself to watching us in silence, watching us and the gendarmes, somewhat disturbed by the strange atmosphere reigning in the coach and the feverish glances we kept casting all round us to seek out the friends, the 'tough guys', who were to identify themselves in the course of the journey.

We were travelling in a cattle truck, sitting on benches in almost total darkness. (The air raids had brought most of the passenger trains to a standstill between the smashed bridges.)

'It' was due to take place at the first cut in the line, the gendarmes had said. 'They' were to follow the train by car.

This was true. 'They' were indeed following the train by car. We had seen them. Furthermore, none of the other passengers could have failed to notice them. They were following, taking such care not to appear to be doing so that they kept passing the slow convoy on the straight stretches; but their conscience prompted them to stop and wait for it at each level-crossing, as though they were afraid of losing it; then they would set off again in pursuit.

The tension mounted inside the coach, in which a tiny oil lamp glimmered. We still kept peering intently at the other passengers, trying to discover our accomplices. Suddenly and spontaneously we all felt certain we had spotted one (and almost certainly a leading one, the brains of the plot) in a mysterious figure sitting astride a bench who never took his eyes off us for a moment.

Never was tough guy or gangster better portrayed in Hollywood. He was dressed with a studied care that reeked of gangsterdom a mile off, with a silk scarf wound round his neck and a broad-brimmed felt hat pulled down over his forehead. He never took his eyes off us except to dart a glance over his shoulder from time to time, no doubt to make sure his shock troops were ready. He kept buttoning and unbuttoning his jacket in a negligent, far too negligent manner—a jacket which in the half light seemed to swell here and there with encouraging bulges. Like us, the gendarmes had recognised him (it would have been impossible not to). We did our utmost to attract his attention and show we had identified him, clearing our throats, furtively turning on our flashlights— maneuvers which inevitably began to intrigue the other passengers. But he just went on sitting there, impassive and enigmatic as ever, like a real man of action, like the Boss.

Nevertheless, there was still a little job for us to do. We had to put the Sûreté inspector to sleep.

We had to slip him the Mickey Finn. Heaven preserve us prisoners and gendarmes, in our agitated state of mind, heaven preserve one of us from drinking the noxious brew by mistake! One of the gendarmes suggested a round of coffee in a trembling voice and with the same sort of ingenuous air as Macbeth must have assumed before murdering King Duncan. The inspector agreed. He was feeling more and more uncomfortable and needed a stimulant. The gendarme produced his mug and the thermos flask. I leaned forward on the pretext of helping him. I uncorked the little phial in the darkness and poured the contents into the mug, praying to heaven that the lurching of the train would not make me spill it all over the floor. Everything went off all right. The gendarme filled the mug up with coffee and handed it to the inspector. The inspector tasted it. Just a sip, to begin with. He didn't pull a face. A second sip, then a third. He went on drinking till he had drained the mug. He had taken the Mickey Finn.

He had taken it. And all of us, prisoners and gendarmes alike, sat panting with curiosity and excitement. Was he going to fall unconscious straight away? Would he begin by yawning, then nod off and gradually fall asleep? We all cast a questioning glance at the man in the scarf and felt hat, the Boss, to whom this sort of business must have held no secrets. He went on sitting there as impassively as ever, but we could see a glint of approval in his eyes.

He had taken it. Ten minutes went by, then a quarter of an hour, during which the tension mounted several degrees higher. To begin with, we forced ourselves to remain calm. One of the gendarmes even made a superhuman effort to appear as impassive and innocent as possible. He curled up on his bench, with his head buried in his arms, and pretended to be fast asleep, the rhythmic sound of his snores drowning the rattling of the coach. No doubt he thereby hoped to induce the enemy to sleep, by contagion. Wasted effort; the latter still sat bolt upright in his seat. So, since neither our composure nor the snoring appeared to yield any result, we began to lose patience and to flash our flashes more and more frequently in the wretch's face, looking feverishly for the first signs of somnolence.

He had taken it. But he had no wish to sleep, I assure you, no, not the slightest wish in the world, poor young man! These tense faces peering into his, these beams of light sweeping over him every moment, these exasperated whispers in the dark had turned his discomfort to agony. It was obvious he thought he was dealing with a lot of lunatics. Never, never had he felt so awake. Never had he been so much on his guard. He had taken it, and more than half an hour had elapsed without his showing the least signs of drowsiness. Labussière was almost weeping with rage and kept fingering the cosh he had concealed under his shirt. The Boss remained impassive and withdrawn. In the dark, on the Mandarin Road, the car continued carefully and loyally to follow the train.

Now we reached the first cut in the line, the first bridge destroyed by the American Air Force. The car had passed the train some time before and was no doubt waiting for us there. We climbed out of the coach and all the passengers made their way towards the emergency footbridge to cross the river and get into another convoy on the opposite bank. The man in the scarf and felt hat was one of the first on his feet and we all gazed at him, waiting for a signal. But he merely lit another cigarette and climbed down onto the line at his leisure. There he was greeted by two men in civilian clothes, who saluted him.

'Good evening, Monsieur le Résident.'

After a final moment of hope, during which we sought to discern a recognition signal in these words, we had to face the facts. This man was really only a civil servant, a genuine civil servant who was returning to his post after a journey, and had nothing whatsoever to do with our business. He was not in the know—not by a long shot. We had made a mistake and our exasperation increased. No friend had yet identified himself.

Yet the mysterious car was there. It wasn't a dream. It had drawn up in front of the damaged bridge. One of the gendarmes went off and discreetly made contact with its occupants. Never would there be a better chance than this. In the almost total darkness, with the crowd jostling round the footbridge, we could easily give the inspector the slip. The gendarme came back after a moment or two. Contact had been established and he repeated the instructions he had received.

'Patience. They're attending to you. It's impossible here, but it will take place at the next cut in the line.'

Very well. Reluctantly we resigned ourselves to climbing into the second train, which then steamed off towards the north. Once again we embarked on the farce of trying to discern the faces of our accomplices in the cattle truck. The Sûreté inspector, still wide awake, asked for some more coffee, then started whistling an odd, irritating little tune.

One of the gendarmes, tired out by these unaccustomed adventures, eventually dozed off, but all of a sudden awoke with a start and turned indignantly on his neighbour, a little weed of a man who had sat down next to him after changing trains but was taking up much too much room and had just stepped on his toe.

'Damn it all, watch what you're doing!'

He had yelled in a parade-ground voice, instinctively fuming at this clumsiness. All the occupants of the coach had turned towards him, which appeared to mortify the weedy little man. He made desperate signs to keep the gendarme quiet, but the latter refused to be mollified.

'Stop shoving, damn it all! There's room enough for us all, isn't there? You don't happen to own this train by any chance, do you?'

Not a hope. The train was not owned by the weedy little man, but the little man was unquestionably one of the friends we were expecting, one of the 'tough guys', one of the accomplices. For the last quarter of an hour at least he had been trying to attract the gendarme's attention, by nudging him with his elbow, and, as a last resort, stamping on his toe, in order to pass him a message. The little man now looked positively sheepish in the beams of the flashlights and under the amused and curious glances fixed on him in the hopes of an altercation. He was even so flustered that he had not the presence of mind to conceal the note he was trying to pass, which could be seen protruding from his breast pocket like the corner of a white handkerchief. More mystified than ever, the Sûreté inspector observed this scene with his eyes standing out as if on stalks.

The gendarme had taken his cue and was now silent. The fuss gradually died down. The inspector started whistling his interminable little tune again. We were able to exchange a few words with our friend in the dark. The friend whispered to us:

'Patience, be calm. Don't get rattled. We're attending to you.'

Then he passed us the note protruding from his pocket. With infinite precautions we deciphered it by the light of a flash. The message ran: 'Don't get rattled. Patience. We're attending to you.'

They were attending to us, all right, there was no doubt about it. A second, even more mysterious car had taken over from the first, and in its turn was following the train like a faithful dog. Then another enigmatic passenger established contact in the dark. Finally, one of the railway employees sidled up to us and murmured:

'Patience. Be calm. We're attending to you. It will take place at the second cut in the line.'

Nothing happened at the second cut in the line, or at the next. By this time the night was almost over and day was beginning to break over the magnificent coast of Annam.

'I know what I'm going to do,' Labussière hissed between his teeth, nodding towards the Sûreté inspector, who was now more and more awake. 'Hit him over the head and chuck him out of the door. Then "they" will be faced with a *fait accompli*.'

In the end he gave up this plan, which was probably as good as any other. We went on waiting and nothing happened.

Nothing happened in the course of the whole journey which, I think, lasted three nights. The conspirators melted away after the second cut in the line and the mysterious cars disappeared. We arrived at Vinh. It was from here, according to the official programme, that we were to be taken by truck to a new prison in Laos. We climbed down from the train. We were greeted with almost military honours by an inspector of the Native Guards, who gave us a wink and murmured under his breath:

'Patience. I'm attending to you. And I'm not the only one. You won't be going to Laos; there's a perfect excuse. All the road bridges have been cut and no truck can get across.'

And he added, with a little chuckle:

'It's not just by chance. The P.W.D. engineers are making *quite sure* they aren't repaired too quickly. You understand? Meanwhile you'll be quartered in a villa by the sea, with the gendarmes and the Sûreté inspector. It's a pretty little place, with a lovely beach.'

In a villa by the sea!

We moved into this villa by the sea with the gendarmes and the Sûreté inspector, who was now completely out of his depth. It was a sumptuous place, about ten miles outside Vinh, on the truly magnificent beach of Cuao-Lo. It normally served as a rest house for V.I.P.s. The Resident's assistant came to make sure we had everything we needed.

We did indeed have everything we needed, so much so that we sometimes felt almost ashamed. We had everything we needed during the four weeks we spent in this seaside resort, which we found quite charming at first, since we expected to stay there only a few days. After our years in prison, the fresh air, the sunshine, the sea bathing and the walks on the beach could not fail to enchant us. We started to get a little colour back in our cheeks. The gendarmes were likewise delighted with this holiday and even the Sûreté inspector began to revel in it. Nothing surprised him any longer, neither our sumptuous quarters, nor the delicious meals prepared for us by a first-class cook, nor our long strolls along the beach, nor even the sight of us wandering off to shoot the waterfowl which abounded in the lagoon, in the company of one of the gendarmes, a real enthusiast, who had brought his gun with him and let us use it now and then. He had grown philosophical, had the inspector. He had fallen into our habit of taking a dip in the sea, then doing a little physical training before lazing on the sand.

This blissful life went on for quite a time. The Resident's

assistant would pass us notes in cipher to keep up our morale, each of these messages enjoining us to have patience, reassuring us that 'they' were attending to us and that 'it' would take place very soon. All the same, after three weeks of this régime, we found it began to pall. We grew impatient again. We started by protesting politely, then we lost our tempers. We sent a letter *en clair* through one of the assistant's agents, addressed to the unknown men in charge of the operation, telling them that if they didn't come and fetch us within the next week we were going to push off on our own through the forest, after first knocking out the Sûreté inspector.

This letter was read in Hué by a friend of Labussière's, André Lan, one of the original instigators of the plot, who had been away on a mission to China, believing this simple operation had been carried out long ago. Lan consulted two other friends, Tisserand and Dassier, and they decided to take immediate action. They commandeered two cars and calmly drove up one evening to the vicinity of Cuao-Lo beach. Lan managed to contact Labussière and told him:

'We'll come and fetch you this evening at midnight.'

Labussière replied:

'Good, we'll be ready.'

So we left at midnight that evening, taking the gendarmes with us. We drove all night without encountering a Japanese road-block and arrived at Hanoi next morning.

As for the Sûreté inspector, he was no bother at all. We left him all alone in the sumptuous villa by the sea, sleeping the sleep of the just. His demeanour had altered completely since the night in the train. He had shed his complexes and nerviness. Tanned by the sea air and having put on a bit of weight, he had fallen into the habit of going to bed every evening at nine o'clock and sleeping ten hours on end, no matter what noise we made in the villa; sleeping like a log, without moving, sleeping the sound heavy sleep procured by an orderly life divided between rest and physical exercise, healthy ample food, an absence of worry and the open air.

We entered Hanoi, driving along the embankments to avoid any possible road-block. There we split up for the time being, for reasons of security. Robert and Labussière were looked after by some civilians for the few days they were to stay in Hanoi. I was put in the care of the military. And there I had a fresh surprise, one of the last in this series of adventures, the biggest of all, perhaps, but one of the most pleasant. A colonel said to me: 'There's an old friend of yours in the next room.' I went in and found de Langlade.

I had left 'Long' on the banks of the Nam-Na. At Hanoi I re-encountered Governor de Langlade: de Langlade who, after spending some time in Europe, had come back with enhanced authority and more extensive powers to this Indo-China of which he had never ceased to dream; de Langlade who, after being parachuted into Tonkin, had made contact with various supporters, old and new, and worked like a demon to organise them into a single coherent body (which was a gigantic task) and channel their activity in the most useful direction; de Langlade, who was disguised at this moment as a mere captain for a clandestine visit to Hanoi, but was saluted with deference by generals who addressed him as 'Major'; de Langlade who, as Delegate of the Provisional Government in the Far East, had just had an interview with the Governor General to inform him of the orders of Free France. There were still some pleasant things in life, even though those orders were not to be carried out to the letter.

Free French Headquarters were at Calcutta, to which we were due to be posted. I was to leave first, next day, while Labussière and Robert would probably follow a week later with de Langlade, who shortly had to rejoin his base. I left Hanoi in an ambulance plane with a young subaltern who was going to Calcutta on a commando course. We landed in Laos on an isolated and deserted airstrip which was used for clandestine operations.

The same evening, at dusk, the sound of an engine which I had been anxiously expecting disturbed the silence of the plateau. The recognition signals were made. An English aircraft came down through the clouds, landed, disembarked some passengers and cases of equipment while we jumped into the fuselage, then took off again. The whole operation had taken no more than a few minutes. The crew were English, all right, and very young. Tears came into my eyes as we flew off towards China. We arrived in the dark at Kunming, without having encountered a single Japanese aircraft, and landed on a huge American aerodrome which seemed to have sprung out of the ground in the last two years. There were aircraft taking off or landing every other minute.

The English gave me an R.A.F. uniform, my last disguise. I spent the night at Kunming and left again next morning for Calcutta in another aircraft. There I rejoined the planters Léonard and d'Iribarne, who were in charge of the Indo-China Intelligence Section. We celebrated my liberation. I must confess I felt completely out of my element, unnerved by the bustle of the huge dusty city teeming with uniforms of every nationality, and paradoxically gloomy and depressed—which I had never felt in prison. I spent a week in an absolute daze waiting for the others to arrive. They eventually turned up, two days later than expected.

We celebrated their liberation as well and they told me about a final incident which worthily rounded off the ups and downs of our escape. Since there was no aircraft available to take them from Hanoi to the airstrip in Laos, they had travelled by car: a final journey of five hundred miles. By a strange coincidence, they had chosen the very route which we had been supposed to take after arriving by train at Vinh. Somewhere along this road they had had to stop because of a damaged bridge which had not yet been repaired. There, the man in charge of the works peered at them intently. He remained immersed in thought for some time, then took Labussière aside and after a moment's hesitation said:

'Excuse me, but aren't you Monsieur Labussière?'

Labussière, equipped of course with false papers, paused

before replying but quickly realised this man was a friend. He was indeed a friend. He was the famous P.W.D. official who had been doing his utmost for over a month *not* to repair the bridges along the road so as to prevent our transfer to the Laos Prison and facilitate our escape. Since no one had informed him this was no longer necessary, he was still fulfilling his mission conscientiously: too conscientiously—they had had to work like slaves for over twenty-four hours to put the cars onto some makeshift rafts and ferry them across the river, the last obstacle that now stood between them and freedom.

At this point I shall end my account of these eventful, often absurd adventures such as certain times of trouble occasionally provoke in lives hitherto devoid of excitement. What happens after the tumultuous elation of the turmoil depends on the intensity of the emotions experienced, on the degree to which the mind has been affected and on the particular manner in which each individual reacts to the return to normality, his ears still buzzing at night with persistent memories. Some, incurably intoxicated by the philter they have drunk, try for all they are worth to prolong the spell. They rush with a sort of desperation in pursuit of further adventures, more often than not to be disappointed, in a period of renewed peace that does not lend itself to this quest. Others, the greater number, recover, either willingly or reluctantly, the equilibrium of normal life. This is what I personally tried to do. I came back to France after an absence of nine years and, after a long spell of leave, returned to Malaya where a pleasant career awaited me, an organisation that afforded less and less room for flights of fancy and a guaranteed pension at the end of so many years. It so happened that I was unable to follow this sensible course. Was it the memory of the Burma Road, of the Nam-Na rapids, or perhaps the endless hours of meditation spent in solitary confinement that had made regular employment seem flat and uninteresting? I had become incapable of doing an ordinary job. For a long time I refused to admit this fact; I struggled against it and tortured myself, until it finally dawned on me one day with startling clarity. After that I felt relieved. The gleam of hope I had been vaguely glimpsing for months, without being able to define the source, suddenly appeared to me with blazing distinctness, like a marvellous beacon re-creating a world of magic and spells.

I made up my mind in an hour, in the course of a sleepless night, with the fireflies darting about more erratically than usual and emitting an unwonted glow in the brushwood round my bungalow ... How could I have hesitated a moment longer? How could I have been so idiotic as to shilly-shally all this time? Was I not clearly appointed by Destiny to make a name for myself in Literature? In the state of mind in which I found myself at this moment, a subtle cocktail of passion and lucidity composed of the radiance of the jungle and the nagging of an obsession rooted deep in the past, I feverishly recapitulated the pressing reasons that impelled me along this course.

In the first place, I had had a scientific education. I had a bent for mathematics, theoretical physics, astronomy and, above all, cosmology. Secondly, I had started life as an electrical engineer, then I had been a rubber planter. Finally, my knowledge of literature was mediocre, almost non-existent as far as contemporary authors were concerned. I had not progressed much further than Anatole France. I read very little, and novels not at all. Essays bored me to tears ... I tell you, it would have been crazy to hesitate a moment longer. It was an instant revelation. This was the course I had to take, and at once, without waiting another second.

It took me no more than three or four days to put this glorious scheme into effect. Once I had made up my mind, I sat down straight away and wrote a letter of resignation to the company for which I worked. I remember this letter clearly; I took infinite pains over its construction and style. I felt as though I were embarking on my literary apprenticeship. The words poured out of their own accord. There was no end to the subtle reasons I found for resigning, to the sarcastic turns of phrase in which I expressed them, so as to produce an 'effect', while I tingled with delight at the thought of the impression my text was bound to make on the directors of the company. It was a promising sign: I was already almost a writer. I redrafted my letter at least half a dozen times, having to make a considerable effort to keep it to a reasonable length befitting its purpose.

After that I got into my car and drove across the peninsula from north to south, stopping at Kuala Lumpur for a bare minute or two to say good-bye to my friends. I took the plane at Singapore, got back to Paris, moved into a little hotel on the Left Bank and started writing a novel, having taken the ridiculous vow to undertake nothing else ever again and having calculated, after selling everything I possessed, that I could live like this for two years, restricting myself to bare essentials.

I have kept my word. I have done practically nothing else ever since, and this foolhardy decision, taken some twenty years ago among the fireflies piercing the equatorial darkness of a Malayan plantation, still strikes me today as the worthy conclusion to a series of incongruous adventures.